HIGH PRAISE FOR

FIRE IN THE SOUL

OTHER BOOKS BY JOAN BORYSENKO

On Wings of Light
Minding the Body, Mending the Mind
Guilt Is the Teacher, Love Is the Lesson

JOAN BORYSENKO, PH.D., is the president of Mind/Body Health Sciences, Inc., and the author of several books including the *New York Times* bestseller *Minding the Body, Mending the Mind* and *Guilt Is the Teacher, Love Is the Lesson*. She co-founded and is a former director of the Mind/Body Clinic at New England Deaconess Hospital and was an Instructor in Medicine at Harvard Medical School. One of the architects of the new medical synthesis called psychoneuroimmunology, Dr. Borysenko is herself a cell biologist, a licensed psychologist, and an instructor in yoga and meditation.

Joan Borysenko, Ph.D.

FIRE IN THE SOUL

A NEW PSYCHOLOGY OF SPIRITUAL OPTIMISM

WARNER BOOKS

A Time Warner Company

Warner Books, Inc., 1271 Avenue of the Americas, New York, NY 10020

ⓦ A Time Warner Company

Printed in the United States of America
First Trade Printing: July 1994
10 9 8 7 6
Originally published in hardcover by Warner Books.

Library of Congress Cataloging-in-Publication Data
Borysenko, Joan.
Fire in the soul: a new psychology of spiritual optimism / Joan
Borysenko.
p.   c.m.
ISBN 0-446-67015-4
1. Spiritual life. 2. Fear—Religious aspects. 3. Peace of mind—
Religious aspects. 4. New Age movement. 1. Title.
BL624.B6195 1993
248.8'6—dc20   92-50521
CIP

Book design by Giorgetta Bell McRee

Cover design by Diane Luger

Illustration by Vivienne Fleisher

For our children,

Andrei, Justin and Natalia Borysenko

And in loving memory of

Mathew Hitchcock

A WORD OF THANKS

My heartfelt thanks go particularly to those people who allowed me to come into their lives—and who enriched my own—by sharing their stories. Yvonne Drew, Thomas Hitchcock, Lee Brunner, Donna Elsten, Fritz Doherty, Tricia Lovett Stallman, Alvin Stallman, Robin Casarjian, Elena Burton, Elizabeth Lawrence and Magaly Rodriguez Mossman. I felt close to each one of you as I wrote.

Thanks, too, to my family—my children, Andrei, Justin and Natalia, and my husband, Myrin—for allowing me to present some of their experiences and for their support and patience during the eighteen months when I locked myself in the study, writing, between trips away from home. Both my parents, Lillian and Edward Zakon, have passed on. Nonetheless, I am grateful to them both and hope they would have appreciated my sharing some of my childhood and adult experiences that involved them in order to help others. My big brother, Alan, helped me more than he knows when I was a child, and his purchases of my books are probably why they've sold so well!

Thanks also to those unnamed people who have shared their stories with me either as patients or as friends. Whenever I have enclosed a person's name in quotes, the story either is a fictional composite drawn from real stories but with no resemblance to any one person's experience or has been altered sufficiently to render the person unrecognizable. In all cases I hope that the dignity, integrity and courage of each person has been preserved.

Thanks to my colleagues. Dr. Rachel Naomi Remen's remarkable insight and clarity have enriched my thinking, as have the bright, fresh ideas of our good friend Larry Dossey, M.D., about "nonlocal mind" and the power of the unconscious. I gratefully acknowledge Herbert Benson, M.D., whose scholarship helped open the door between medicine and spirituality. Jon Kabat-Zinn, Ph.D., who was the original "fairy godfather" of the mind/body program that I directed during much of the 1980s, taught me a great deal about mindfulness meditation. Dr. Willis Harman's thinking about science and metaphysics has been a substantial influence, as has the work of other colleagues far too numerous to mention. When appropriate, I have acknowledged your contributions in the text. To any of you whose work I have drawn upon but whose name I haven't mentioned specifically, thank you, for none of us stands alone. Every book and article is built on the thinking of countless others.

A very special thanks to Stephen Maurer for introducing me to Tolstoy's story "The Three Questions" and for the love he gave me during the most trying time of my life; to Rick Ingrasci and Peggy Taylor for their friendship and encouragement, and for introducing me to the power of community healing circles; to Robin Casarjian for ploughing through the manuscript in its awkward stages and encouraging some important changes and—when I had reached the point of absolute desperation at the end of this long labor—delivering me a title; to Peggy Taylor for her insightful comments about reorganizing the manuscript; and to Irene Borge for introducing me to the work of Victor Turner.

An extra special thanks to the mystical, magical Mother Goose—Celia Thaxter Hubbard, whose friendship, encouragement and love have meant the world to me. Both her research, which yielded a steady stream of books and articles from seminal thinkers, and her own good counsel have enriched this book tremendously and helped convert me to spiritual optimism. The cover image was inspired by one of Celia's own creations. Her love of art and beauty has been a continuing source of education and inspiration.

To the Circle of Women: Celia Hubbard, Joan Drescher, Carolina Clark, Peggy Taylor, Elizabeth Lawrence, Yvonne Drew, Rachel Naomi Remen, Tricia Lovett Stallman, Leslie Kussman, Loretta Laroche, Lauren Macintosh, Renee Summers, Elena Burton, Robin Casarjian, Olivia Hoblitzelle, Jane Alter, Magaly Rodriguez Mossman—I can't express how much you all mean to me and how our shared experience has helped to shape this book and add joy to my life.

And last, but certainly not least, thanks to the two people who made this book a reality. My wonderful literary agent, Helen Rees, and my exceptional editor at Warner Books, Joann Davis. Thank you both for your faith in me and for giving me the opportunity to say my peace.

CONTENTS

Contents

This is a book about freedom,
about breaking the chains of old beliefs and fears
that keep us in bondage to the illusion
that we are separate from each other and from
All That Is.

Freedom is the destiny of every living being.
We become free by waking from our
dreams of fear, scarcity, blame and guilt,
by taking responsibility for acting,
to the best of our knowledge,
with care and loving-kindness that we may
kindle the light of love within and
by that light see our way home
and serve as beacons for others along the way.

It is most often suffering that kindles love,
loss that deepens understanding,
hurt that opens the eyes of the heart
that see forgiveness as a way of life and
peace of mind as our birthright.

J.Z.B.

PART ONE

Basic Beliefs— The Choice for Love or Fear

---

*We do not see things as they are.
We see them as we are.*

—The Talmud

INTRODUCTION

The Fire of Transformation

What the caterpillar calls the end of life,
the master calls a butterfly.

Richard Bach

I have lived and breathed this book for years, struggling with questions of meaning in a world where negative events often seem random—or worse, cruel. Both in my practice as a medical psychologist and in my personal life my soul has burned with the question *why*? If there is any goodness in this universe, why do human beings suffer? Are we tainted by original sin? Are we living out our karma? Is there a personal God who punishes us? Or do our very wounds contain the seeds of an individual, or even planetary, awakening to a state of greater wisdom, compassion, creativity and love?

I had thought to find the answer to these questions in studying philosophy, religion and psychology. But I have been tutored most poignantly by my own trials and by those of friends, family and clients in my professional capacity as a medical psychologist, educator and workshop leader. This book is extraordinarily special to me not only because it presents a new and much needed psychology of spiritual optimism—the point of view that every difficult experience provides an opportunity for soul growth and spiritual homecoming—but also because it is intensely personal. In reading it you will meet my teachers, people with whom I have been both on the giving and receiving end of deep and transformative healing.

My friend, Lee, for example was living with AIDS for most of the time I was writing this book. Just after it was completed, Lee's physical condition deteriorated and I went to visit him, heavyhearted that my friend was so close to death. I had hoped to comfort and perhaps even inspire him, yet it was Lee who gave me comfort. I went into his bedroom and lay my head on his chest. We hugged wordlessly. When I sat up, our eyes met and we remained in silent communion for half an hour or more. I have never felt so much love. It seemed that all of the suffering Lee endured had burned away the masks, the veils, the insecurities that keep us out of touch with our own holiness. When the burning was done, his inner light shone unobstructed. I have never been on holier ground.

When our souls are on fire, old beliefs and opinions can be consumed, bringing us closer to our essential nature and to the heart of healing. These times of inner burning have been called dark nights of the soul. The Spanish mystic, St. John of the Cross, coined that term in the mid–1500's. He used it to designate that part of the spiritual journey during which we seem to lose our connection with an inner source of peace and instead confront our deepest fears and pains. St. John saw suffering as a "purgative" administered by the divine light to cleanse the soul of all residue that would keep it separate and alone.

Poet/philosopher Kahlil Gibran had another definition of pain. He viewed it as "the bitter pill of the inner physician," a kind of wake-up call from the Universe that "breaks the shell of our understanding." This book is about the newness that can emerge in our souls when that shell is broken; the freedom to be ourselves and the awakening to a whole new dimension of life—the spiritual.

Mythologist Joseph Campbell described this process of awakening as a terrifying night-sea journey, and indeed it can be frightening because in times of extreme suffering it can seem as though all our moorings have torn away and we are floating alone in uncharted waters. In order to find our way home we need a guide. Otherwise we might get lost in a sea of depression, despair, cynicism, help-lessness or addiction. This book is meant to be such a guide. But more than that, it is meant to help you find your own inner guid-ance.

On a personal note, this was a very difficult and also exciting book to write. It came directly from the fire in my own soul, a deep passion for freedom, transformation and spiritual homecoming whose flames have long been fed by my arch-nemesis and greatest teacher—fear. At times my fear has gotten the better of me, literally burning me up and burning me out. But as the mythical phoenix, I have always resurrected as have so many of the clients I have been privileged to work with over the years. The ways in which fear and trauma are transformed into insight and compassion are incredibly fascinating and have led me to look beyond the boundaries of our traditional psychological systems.

Early in my career as a psychologist I was a behaviorist. I believed that needless psychological suffering could be relieved by teaching people a new set of behaviors and beliefs. And, indeed, behavioral and cognitive-behavioral therapy is extremely useful in some circum-stances as I discuss in my first book, *Minding the Body, Mending the Mind*. Later in my career I became aware of the importance of healing the wounds of childhood and recovering self-esteem as I discuss in my second book, *Guilt Is the Teacher, Love Is the Lesson*. In the present book, we will move even more deeply into the nature of healing, considering a spiritual psychology in which the wholeness of a person comprises not just their temporal mind but their immortal soul.

Although psychology technically means the study of the soul, most psychological systems abandoned any interest in soul in their bid to be "scientific." Thus the remarkable teachings of Swiss psychiatrist Carl Jung and Italian psychiatrist Roberto Assagioli, both of whom recognized the importance of the soul, were overshadowed by the work of their contemporary, Sigmund Freud. While Freud had a great deal to say about the personal unconscious, his theories neglected the collective unconscious posited by Jung—the realm of the archetypes or soul patterns like healer, warrior, magician and hero that have informed myth, theater, religions and the dream world since the beginnings of time.

The limited scope of traditional psychology has been stunningly revealed over the past decade by breakthroughs in our understanding of trauma, as we will discuss in Part Two: The Transformation of Fear. Many people who are severely traumatized develop what are called "dissociative disorders." They space out mentally to distance themselves from abuse and terror, and in so doing learn to function in alternate realities. They may develop multiple personality disorder, and while such people can be severely limited by their unhealed pain, they may also develop exceptional intuitive and creative abilities.

In the majority of multiples, therapists can locate a core personality, called the Inner Self Helper, that seems to be the soul. Regardless of the person's religious upbringing or lack thereof, the Inner Self Helper claims to be an immortal core of consciousness that was present before the person had a body and will remain present when their body dies. It often characterizes itself as a conduit for divine love and wisdom. And it is wise. This personality can be very helpful to the therapist in transforming the trauma that led to such severe fragmentation of self.

As I travel across the country giving workshops for therapists and for the general public, I hear remarkable stories from and about people who were severely abused as children. Many of them connect with the Inner Self Helper during the process of healing, and the majority are highly intuitive. Many of them have memories of extraordinary spiritual experiences that accompanied their abuse. When long-repressed memories of abuse surface as part of their healing, the spiritual experiences also surface. They tend to be of two types: out-of-body experiences and meeting with a white light similar to the all-wise, all-loving light people report as part of near-death experiences.

Lynne Finney, a lawyer and therapist who is herself a survivor of severe sexual abuse and torture, recounts her own experience and those of many clients in her remarkable book, *Reach for the Rainbow:*

Advanced Healing for Survivors of Sexual Abuse. She comments that memories of the white light are often surprising both to clients, who may be overtly atheistic, and to therapists who have not encountered such things previously. Lynne remarks that:

> The reports generally have similar features: the victim sees a white light which begins to grow larger and brighter. The victim knows instantly that the white light is a power for good and love and understands what the white light is saying even though it does not actually speak. The light informs the victim that the victim is loved, that there is a reason for what is happening and that the victim will survive the abuse. Some victims are given elaborate information about the universe and their lives and futures. Victims report feeling intense love and peace in the presence of the light unlike anything they have known before. (*Reach for the Rainbow*, p. 189)

I have personally heard dozens of such stories that my traditional psychological training left me unprepared for. Clients' accounts of the white light, of near-death experiences, of angelic intervention, of past-life recall and even of UFO abduction can no longer be summarily dismissed as hysteria, psychosis or flawed character. These phenomena are real and very commonplace. Interestingly, persons who were traumatized as children are more likely than the remainder of the population to have access to altered states of consciousness and other realities as we will discuss in Part Two. Nonetheless, research from the National Social Survey indicates that spiritual experiences overall are associated with excellent mental health. And indeed, some of the healthiest people I know are those who have had to heal from the most challenging situations, and in the process, have gained insight and wisdom far beyond what a "comfortable" life would ordinarily provoke.

I have experienced a number of childhood traumas, despite the fact that I was raised in a caring home environment. At the age of ten I developed a severe mental illness, obsessive-compulsive disor-

der, that you will read about in Chapter Three: Crisis as Initiation.
Developing this illness was like waking up one morning in hell and
finding that there was no exit. But in the process of recovering—
entirely without human help although I believe that I had tremendous
help from the angelic realm—I discovered my Inner Self Helper and
the white light. I also developed the ability to move in and out of
altered states of consciousness with some ease.

Although initially I had no framework for understanding the sudden onset and miraculous healing from that devastating mental illness, I now view it as an initiation experience into the sisterhood/
brotherhood of healers. Jung spoke of the archetype called the
wounded healer. I believe that each wound we suffer and eventually
heal from is a soul-making experience with the potential to awaken
our willingness to participate in the healing of our world.

We are living in an unprecedented time. The world soul is truly
on fire with hunger, pollution and hatred. Many of us are wounded.
And it is up to each person to use the fire of their wounds consciously—to heal, to work for peace, to transform our world. If we
do not, the fire in our souls will burn us up both individually and
collectively. Our cities will burn, our children will turn to drugs,
our earth will become too polluted to sustain life. More and more
people—paradoxically through pain, abuse and trauma—are literally seeing the light and committing themselves to personal
and societal healing. To be healers we need to go beyond being
victims or even survivors of whatever our own private hell might
be. We are being called upon instead to become transformers of
consciousness.

In dealing with the difficult challenges of this lifetime, door-
ways to other realities and other lifetimes may open that occasion a
deeper healing than our previous religious or philosophical beliefs
may have conditioned us to expect. My own clinical experience has
convinced me that this lifetime is one drop in a much larger bucket.
As Donna Elsten, about whose stunning near-death experience you
will read in Chapter Two, puts it, "Our life on earth is like a flash of
lightning." A snap of the fingers and we awaken from the dream. But
the experience stored in our souls, our deeper identity, stays with us

in other realms of existence. And we grow and heal on many levels simultaneously.

Through this expanded view of life even the most painful and seemingly senseless events can be understood as grist for the mill of soul-making and deep healing. Despite the challenges we face, help is reliably available from the universe when we ask for it—although it may not fit our criteria for the help we had in mind. I have come to believe wholeheartedly that we are eternally and immortally safe, even though the temporal world in which we live is often dangerous, violent and unpredictable. This is spiritual optimism. I have organized this book in a way that will help you to reflect on your own experiences and beliefs, as well as presenting you with both an intellectual and experiential framework for a new psychology of spiritual optimism.

Part One presents the choice we make in every time of crisis: to believe in love or to capitulate to fear. The first three chapters lay a basic psychological, scientific, religious and spiritual framework for our beliefs about why bad things happen that I hope will help you to identify your own thinking patterns. Part Two addresses both the personal and archetypal fears that become particularly obvious in times of crisis, but that many of us experience chronically. When should we consider meditation versus medication, traditional therapy versus transpersonal approaches like past-life regressions? What is the most comprehensive psychology of love, courage and freedom that can give us safe passage through fear?

Part Three presents practical strategies for courageous living that allow us to experience our daily lives with peace, joy and freedom. The English word "courage" comes from the French *coeur*, meaning "heart." Meditation, prayer, and mindfulness of what is—these are ways that we open the eyes of the heart in order to see clearly when a dark night of the soul obscures our vision. The book concludes with a resource section that lists books, tapes and addresses of helpful individuals and organizations, preceded by a chapter called "Night Lights," stories, poems and quotations that can help restore spiritual optimism when it's at a low ebb and we seem to have forgotten how to live with faith, love and courage. And this forgetting and remembering, dear reader, is the pulse of life here on planet earth.

As I have come to say in all my books,

Come and let us remember together.

Joan Borysenko
May 27, 1992
Scituate, MA

A PARABLE:
SAFE PASSAGE HOME

Once upon a time, a long long time ago,
before even
Grandfather Sky had given birth to the stars,
there was only One Being.
One pure consciousness of love resting in the completeness
of its own untold Stories and mute Songs unsung.

Then, one day, for reasons that no one remembers,
if in fact anyone ever knew,
the One became restless.
Some say it decided to play a cosmic game of
hide and seek, splitting its Light into
tiny sparks, each with the full potential of the Whole.
In this way the One could know itself and grow itself.

So each spark was clothed in a costume of flesh
and its Light and wisdom hidden deep within its heart.
The challenge of the game was for all parts of the Whole
to discover their way back Home again
having lived all the Stories and sung all the Songs
that would make them wise and compassionate
co-creators and companions to the One.

The fledgling souls took many roads Home.
Each Way had its own Story and each soul
responded to that Story with the gift of free will,
embroidering new stories on the dream-tapestry
of the One Great Dreamer.
And the sun rose and the sun set.
The tides came in and the tides went out.
New flesh was born and old flesh went back to the earth.
And the One saw new stories grow in the Theater of the Many.

11

Some of these stories led closer to Home.
These were the ones in which fear was conquered by love.
Some of these stories led down blind alleys.
These were the ones in which love was hidden by fear.
The plays were long and the distractions many.
One by one
most souls forgot that they were on a journey at all.
They fell asleep to the First Stories
that the One had left as eternal roadmaps and guides
so that each soul could find its way
back Home.

Believing that they were alone and separate
these lost souls wandered in a strange land
dominated by the illusion that death was real and
that love was as transitory as a shadow.
Some sought solace in money, others in power.
Some found it in food or drugs or alcohol or anger or
television or possessions,
gossip or judgment or a jealous god
who whispered lies. You are special, you are saved,
there is only one way Home and this is it.

In its love and mercy for the lost parts of itself
the One sent alarm bells out into the Universe
to wake its sparks from their dreams of fear
and to guide them back into paths of love and longing
for reunion with the Great Cosmic Beloved.
These wake-up calls of pain roused the souls from their
sleep of forgetfulness.

And their cries for help were heard by their
brothers and sisters throughout the Universe.
Seen and unseen helpers came
whenever they were drawn by the intent,
the powerful pull of will
of any soul who appealed to the Source
with a true longing for reunion, forgiveness and love.
And they helped those souls to become free
from the bondage of limiting beliefs and

past unloving or ignorant actions
so that they could find
safe passage Home.

They will give you safe passage, too,
if you ask with faith,
even the size of a mustard seed,
and if you are patient and willing to listen
to the directions of the Universe,
even if they are
not what you wanted to hear.
Thy will, not mine, be done—
this is the understanding
that will bring you Home.

CHAPTER ONE

Why Do Bad Things Happen?

The only thing that we can know is that we know nothing and that is the highest flight of human wisdom.

Leo Tolstoy

I had almost finished the first draft of this chapter late in June 1990 when a tragedy led our family to ask the age-old question: "Why? If there is any love in this universe, why do bad things happen?"

My husband, Myrin, and I were sound asleep when we awakened with a start at 5:30 in the morning, the way a mother does when her baby begins to cry. Although our "baby," Andrei, was a young man of seventeen, we awakened instantly at his cries of distress. We ran down the hall and burst into his room along with our older son, Justin. Andrei was holding his chest as if his heart had been torn out. He was screaming, "Why? Why? No! No!" as a torrent of tears ran from his sleepy blue eyes down tanned cheeks that had suddenly gone chalk white. Andrei's anguish was so great that it seemed an accusation of life, a challenge to God.

Andrei had just received the phone call I've always feared the most. The one that would tell me that a loved one had died suddenly. His best friend, Mat, had died earlier that night when his car careened out of control on a dangerous, dark curve made slippery by the summer rains. Although an expert team of paramedics helicoptered him to our regional trauma center, Mat died before he even reached the hospital. Andrei's anguished *"why?"* was repeated by most of the teenagers who gathered at our home to grieve during the first few days after the tragedy. Why Mat? Why the one who never had a critical word for anyone, the one who was so grateful for life, so accepting of the uniqueness and potential of everyone he met? "Why the very best of us?" they asked.

At odds with Andrei and the others, one young woman admonished, "Don't even ask that question. It doesn't have an answer that we could possibly understand." This teenager in white sneakers and red socks had put her finger directly on the pulse of the sacred mystery. We cannot know. But for human beings the need to know goes hand in hand with restructuring our world after tragedy.

Tragedy brings forth the need to create meaning—to tell new stories—that can reweave the frayed ends of life into a coherent whole. Our ability to tell these stories is positively linked with recovery, according to the research of UCLA-based psychologist Shelley Taylor. Studying people whose lives had been disrupted by misfortunes that ranged from rape to life-threatening illness, Dr. Taylor found that those who readjusted well incorporated three coping strategies into their recovery: a search for meaning in the experience, an attempt to gain mastery over the event in particular and life in general, and a recouping of self-esteem after they had suffered some loss or setback.

Dr. Taylor was awed by the remarkable resilience of human nature and the deep reservoir of strength that tragedy taps. She observed that, rather than folding in times of crisis, most people have the innate capacity to recover from monumental problems, readjusting to life not only as well as, but even better than, before the tragedy occurred. And the meaning we ascribe to these dark nights of the soul is central to how we emerge from them.

What does it mean to lose a loved one, to get cancer, to be raped at knifepoint, to be molested as a child? If our answers create negative, fearful stories, then recovery from trauma is impeded. Research indicates that people who believe that they are helpless victims are more likely to remain anxious, depressed and angry than people who retain a feeling of control. A helpless, blaming attitude has in turn been linked to decreased immune function, increased heart disease and susceptibility to a whole panoply of stress-related disorders.

Equally paralyzing is self-blame, the pessimistic triad of feelings that University of Pennsylvania psychologist Dr. Martin E. P. Seligman sums up as "It's all my fault, I mess up everything I do, and it's the story of my life." Pessimism compromises immune function, makes it difficult to learn from our experiences and leaves us depressed and powerless. If the stories we weave from our tragedies are more optimistic ("I don't know why this happened, but I can deal with it," or "Someday I'll see the value in this situation," or "I'm already learning from this experience"), then both physical and mental health are optimized.

During the seven years that I directed a mind/body clinical program at Boston's Beth Israel and New England Deaconess hospitals, I had the chance to hear hundreds of "Why me?" stories. Most people came to the clinic at a point in their lives where illness had presented a new and often daunting challenge. Frequently their unquestioned ideas and assumptions about life were shattered by the diagnosis of a life-threatening illness, the reality of living with multiple sclerosis or a head injury, or by the seeming endlessness of fear or depression. The treatment we offered was a group program that met for two hours a week over a ten-week period.

Patients were taught to use mental techniques including meditation and focused imagination that can produce healthful shifts in bodily physiology. They were also trained in the program of stretching, relaxation, self-awareness, breaking the anxiety cycle, reframing the meaning of their experience, exercise and nutrition that I presented in *Minding the Body, Mending the Mind*.

One group of patients in particular is etched in my memory. It was the first session of the ten-week program, and people were explaining why they had come. One woman had migraine headaches so severe that she was afraid of losing her job because of repeated absences from work. Another woman had a neurological disorder that could not be specifically diagnosed. Every time the symptoms of mild disorientation began, she panicked. Was it a brain tumor that had evaded detection? Would the symptoms get worse and make it impossible for her to function? There was a man with chronic back pain and a woman who was an incest survivor with a host of stress-related complaints linked to that childhood trauma. Two others had diarrhea and belly pain from irritable bowel syndrome, and several others suffered from panic attacks accompanied by bodily problems such as high blood pressure or irregular heart beats.

The last person to talk was "Leslie." An attractive, well-groomed brunette in her early forties, Leslie was a single mother who worked in a bank while raising two young daughters. She looked around the circle as she summarized in a soft yet strong voice her reasons for coming. "My husband died about three years ago. He was only thirty-nine, but he had a stroke. He was in Spaulding [a Boston-area rehabilitation hospital] for several months and then he came home. He was partially paralyzed on his right side and couldn't work. But, you know, he had a great attitude. He was happy to be alive." Leslie stopped to blink back the tears and clear her throat before she continued. "Just after dinner one night he had a second stroke and died. Peacefully. And in my arms."

Leslie paused for a moment to collect herself, "I hadn't worked since our two girls, Cindy and Ellen, were born, but after Bob died I got a job in a bank. It was a tough adjustment all around, but we were doing okay. Then about a year later I found a lump in my right breast. It was malignant, and there were three positive lymph nodes—not so many that I feel hopeless, but I also know I'm not out of the woods yet. I've had surgery, radiation and chemotherapy, and now I want to make sure that I'm doing everything I can to recover. I want to live to see my daughters grow up."

There was a stunned silence in the group as people absorbed Leslie's story. "Janet," the woman whose migraines were so disruptive, spoke first. Tears glistened in her eyes as she nodded at Leslie. "My headaches are painful and they make life unpredictable, but when I listened to you I realized how much I have to be grateful for. I'm amazed by your courage."

I was amazed by Leslie's courage, too. When I had first interviewed her so that we could decide together whether a mind/body program was appropriate for her needs, I asked her the same question that I routinely ask patients with potentially serious illness. "Even though most of the time there's no way to know why we get sick, most people have some kind of theory anyway. What about you?"

Leslie smiled, "Do you mean do I ask, 'Why me'?" I nodded, and she continued. "At first I did, but then I figured why not me? How can we really know the reasons why anything happens. Why does some alcoholic child-molester live until eighty-five while babies die? My mother used to tell me that bad things happened to people because they were being punished for their sins, but all you have to do is look around you to see how dumb that theory is! The truth is that I don't know why Bob died and then I got cancer, Joan. All I know for sure, deep in my heart, is that somehow, in some way that I may never understand in this life, it is ultimately for the good." I could hear the sincerity in Leslie's voice that told me she was speaking from her innermost truth, not from some fearful rationalization. I told her so.

"I'm certainly not a fatalistic Pollyanna. I'm scared," she continued. "Some days I shake myself when I wake up, thinking that I'm caught in some awful nightmare." Leslie paused and sighed. "When I realize I'm awake, I have to adjust to this damn cancer, to my loneliness, all over again. I wonder if I'll live a normal lifespan or die young. And if I live I wonder what kind of life I'll have, whether I'll ever fall in love again, whether any man would marry me. And I wonder how it will be for the children if I'm sick, if I die. Then I start to think, 'Well, this is what's happening. This is the role I've been given to play. I'm going to do it as consciously and gracefully as I can.' "

"Jay," a patient I met at about the same time as Leslie, had a radically different attitude. An extremely successful artist from New York, Jay was a gay man in his mid-thirties whose work had garnered national acclaim. Diagnosed with AIDS about six months before we met, Jay had lost some weight but was still working and feeling reasonably good. He had a strong support system of friends, but his emotional state was perilous as a result of his beliefs about why he had AIDS.

When Jay asked himself the question "Why me?" his answer was based on old, unexamined religious beliefs left over from childhood.

Although not religious as an adult, Jay had been raised a Southern Baptist. In his desperation over his own illness and his grief for other friends who were ill or dead from AIDS, Jay regressed to a state of childlike helplessness. His old religious beliefs surfaced with fresh power. He deduced that the Bible was right to condemn homosexuals after all, and, if it was right on that score, then it might follow that he would go to hell for his sexual practices.

Jay was tormented day and night by his guilt. His behavior was like a parody of a fundamentalist tent preacher hurling blame, fear, fire and brimstone at himself. I suggested that Jay seek the help of a minister trained in pastoral counseling to help him separate some of his intrinsic fear and pessimism—the result of being raised in an abusive home—from his fear of God. As I discussed in *Guilt Is the Teacher, Love Is the Lesson,* a person's view of God as loving and merciful as opposed to punitive and judgmental correlates highly with self-esteem. Our self-esteem, in turn, correlates with how we were treated by our parents. If our parents were loving and we grew up feeling worthy and good about ourselves, we feel that God is also good. If our parents were harsh and authoritarian and we grow up feeling bad about ourselves, then we are likely to feel that God is punitive, as our parents were.

Since Jay lived in New York, we saw each other only intermittently on his visits to friends who lived in Boston. One day, after a hiatus of a few months, he came to our session with an armload full of books on self-healing. Jay's helpless, pessimistic attitude had lifted, and he looked strong and vibrant. He told me that he now believed that his self-hatred had created the conditions that made him susceptible to AIDS, and that he should be able to reverse those conditions by loving himself. He had positive affirmations hung all over his house and was deeply engaged in a program of imagery for self-healing.

Frankly, I was worried about him. His sudden shift in attitude seemed like a Band-Aid hastily applied to an open wound. In his misery and psychic pain, Jay had too easily accepted the simplistic notion of being 100 percent responsible for creating his own reality. It gave him a temporary sense of safety. The idea that what we create we can uncreate is one of those partial truths that can be very injurious. At the extreme of this philosophy, all illness is perceived as a failure, and a temporary illusion of power is created by the attitude that we can cure what we have caused.

I encouraged Jay to think about the wide range of alternate answers to the question "Why me?" that lay between the two extremes he had subscribed to thus far. His old beliefs gave God all the power. His new beliefs gave Jay all the power. He left the session upset with my failure to endorse his new point of view. Because my major interest is the intersection of psychology, medicine and spirituality—and because I endorse the constructive use of meditation, affirmation and participation in our own healing—Jay assumed that I would agree with his "New Age" philosophy, a label I abhor because it has been used with so little precision that it is effectively meaningless.

While we certainly participate in creating the events of our lives, the idea that we are 100 percent responsible for creating our own reality is a psychologically and spiritually impoverished notion. In my experience, when patients with this belief are unable to cure themselves, they often feel like failures or undergo a painful crisis of faith. While such crises can be important invitations to deeper healing when there is time to pursue the ramifications, they can be a serious blow for people coping with life-threatening illnesses that may afford neither the time nor the energy to pick up the pieces of a shattered faith.

Every once in a while Jay phoned from New York with a progress report. The symptoms of his AIDS gradually worsened, and, despite the help of a therapist, Jay's psychological state also deteriorated. He felt helpless and unworthy because he had not been able to cure himself physically or to find peace emotionally. When Jay became so weak that he realized death was imminent, his faith in being able to create his own reality crumbled, and he fell back to his original belief that AIDS was a punishment.

Like Leslie and Jay, most of us have faced, or will face, life crises. At that time our basic beliefs about ourselves and the Universe— the sometimes only half-conscious scripts by which we live—will determine how we face our dark nights of the soul. Will they bring us closer to Home or will they drive us into the wilderness of fear and isolation? More than any other question, "Why me?" puts us face to face with what we really believe.

A FIRST STORY

A First Story, as I presented the idea in the parable that opens this section, is an archetype—a master story—that each person must live through in the process of growing their soul and finding their way back to God. For anyone who has ever read the Old Testament, the story of Job is certainly the archetype of "Why me?" It asks the question why, if there is any fairness in the universe, do bad things happen to good people? Job's is one of the oldest stories on record. Scholars believe that it was written between 800 and 300 B.C. and is based on a much older Sumerian version of the legend dating back to about 2000 B.C.

The story of Job concerns a righteous man, according to the Bible the most esteemed man on earth in God's sight. Job is suddenly beset by terrible suffering when Satan asks God to test Job's loyalty. In one day God arranges for all Job's ten children to die, for his vast herds of animals to be killed and finally for Job to be stricken with hideous, painful boils. Job then sits with three friends for a week, fruitlessly debating the question of why bad things happen to good people. As with many biblical stories, the answer is not immediately obvious. It is up to the reader to ferret out the teaching, a process that is very valuable because it makes you think.

After years of thinking about the story of Job, I believe that the parable is best understood not in terms of the question "Why do bad things happen to good people?" but in terms of the question "Do the trials Job suffers deepen his understanding about the nature of God?" According to both the King James and Revised Standard Bibles (the excerpts below are from the Revised Standard version), Job learns nothing from his suffering except that he must repent of even complaining. This thoughtful, righteous man ends up groveling in shame before the awesome power of a tyrannical God. But according to the more meticulous translation of Hebrew scholar and poet Stephen

Mitchell, Job instead has a wondrous, freeing revelation about the true nature of the divine.

ONCE UPON A TIME THERE WAS A MAN NAMED JOB

> *There was a man in the land of Uz whose name was Job; and that man was blameless and upright, one who feared God, and turned away from evil. There were born to him seven sons and three daughters. He had seven thousand sheep, three thousand camels, five hundred yoke of oxen, and five hundred she-asses, and very many servants; so this man was the greatest of all the people in the East.*

The Old Testament narrator's prologue next shifts to God's yearly gathering with the angels, a conclave at which Satan is also present. In the Old Testament, "Satan" is only rarely used (four times, to be exact) to mean a divine being with evil intent. Episcopal priest and Jungian analyst John Sanford, in his excellent book *Evil: The Shadow Side of Reality*, discusses the more common use of "satan," a noun meaning "adversary" or "accuser"; as a verb it means to "persecute by hindering free forward movement." In the secular sense, any kind of pain, illness or loss is a satan with which we must wrestle to discover our wholeness, our authenticity as creative, self-aware human beings.

Sanford points out that in the Old Testament God himself sometimes functions as a satan, performing the necessary job of obstruction so that we must pause to consider our lives in a new light. In the story of Job, Satan and God are two beings on good terms, in collusion with one another. The "Accusing Angel," as Stephen Mitchell translates "Satan" from the Hebrew, informs God that he's been walking around the earth "here and there" checking out what's happening. God immediately wants to know if the Accuser has seen his marvelous servant Job, for *"there is none like him on the earth, a blameless and upright man, who fears God and turns away from evil."*

Satan then lives up to the literal translation of his name. He ponders an important psychospiritual question, really the most important question there is about a human being. Is Job really a holy man, one who knows the completeness of himself and therefore knows God. Or is he just a goody-goody, invested in looking holy, singing God's praises only because his life is sailing along so smoothly? Satan is not suggesting that Job might be evil but rather that he might be unconscious.

Satan is posing the same question that a depth psychologist might ask. Is Job using his talents, expressing his feelings and living his life authentically, or is he simply identifying with an idealized notion of what he thinks a good person is? In the unthinking desire to be "good" we risk disowning all the parts of ourselves—including healthy emotions and talents—that were ever shamed by parents, teachers, clergy or society. Our uniqueness gradually gets relegated to the unconscious, to what C. G. Jung called the shadow, and in the course of growing up we get progressively more identified with the mask or "false self" we wear to get other people's approval. (This process of losing ourselves is discussed in depth in my second book, *Guilt Is the Teacher, Love Is the Lesson.*)

So, Satan's accusation of Job puts his authenticity—his wholeness—to the test, as life does time and time again for each of us. Satan asks God whether Job doesn't have good reason to sing his praises:

Hast thou not put a hedge about him and his house and all that he has, on every side? Thou hast blessed the work of his hands, and his possessions have increased in the land. But put forth thy hand now, and touch all that he has, and he will curse thee to thy face.

God replies to Satan: *"Behold, all that he has is in your power; only upon himself do not put forth your hand."* That same day, Satan arranges the theft and burning of Job's herds, the slaughtering of many of his servants, and the "accidental" deaths of all Job's ten children. Job is the very model of patience and forbearance in the face of this enormous suffering. His only comment is: *"Naked I came from my mother's womb, and naked shall I return: the Lord gave, and the Lord has taken away; blessed be the name of the Lord.*" Job's initial attitude of surrender has given rise to the common expression "to have the patience of Job." An erroneous expression, if you read the rest of the parable.

God is smug with satisfaction at Job's meek response. He says to Satan: "He still holds fast his integrity [Mitchell translates this as *innocence*], although you moved me against him, to destroy him without cause."

But Satan is not at all impressed by Job's initial show of faith. As a well-trained depth psychologist might do, he muses over whether Job is acting from his integrity—his wholeness—or from a false mask of goodness. He presses the question and says to God:

"*Skin for skin! All that a man has he will give for his life. But put forth thy hand now and touch his bone and his flesh, and he will curse thee to thy face.*" And God said to Satan: "*Behold, he is in your power; only spare his life.*"

Satan then covers poor Job's whole body with boils. Job, still manifesting the patience he is unduly famous for, simply sits in the dust, scratching himself with a pottery shard. His wife is less patient: "*Do you still hold fast your integrity [innocence]? Curse God, and die.*"

But cling to his innocence Job does for seven days and seven nights while three friends sit in silence to console him for his terrible losses. Finally Job cries out in anguish;

> Let the day perish wherein I was born and the night which said, a man-child is conceived. . . . Let the stars of its dawn be dark . . . because it did not shut the doors of my mother's womb, nor hide trouble from my eyes . . . . Why did I not die at birth? . . . Why did the knees receive me? Or why the breasts, that I should suck? . . . For the thing that I fear comes upon me, and what I dread befalls me.

Stop for a moment and let the power of those words sink in. Have you ever felt this way? If Job's poetic lament awakened the memory of a dark night of your own, where do you think your suffering came from? Did you ask and answer the question "Why me?" You might like to take a few minutes to reflect upon your experience in writing. We will return to the parable of Job together later in the chapter, after we have had a chance to position, in both a psychological and religious framework, the question of why bad things happen to good people.

PSYCHOLOGICAL AND RELIGIOUS PESSIMISM

A doughnut-shaped greeting card that I once sent to a friend defined optimism and pessimism succinctly. It said, "The difference between an optimist and a pessimist is droll. The optimist sees the doughnut and the pessimist sees the hole." When we get down to our beliefs about why bad things happen, optimists and pessimists indeed see the doughnut differently.

Psychologists classify people as optimists or pessimists based on how they answer the question "Why me?" The pessimist is a helpless sort who explains his plight with three characteristic arguments: internal, stable and global. The pessimist believes: It's all my fault (internal), it's the story of my life (stable) and I mess up everything I do (global).[1] Jay, the AIDS patient whom you read about earlier in this chapter, was a pessimist. Like all pessimists, he tended to be chronically anxious, depressed and guilty since he felt helpless to keep bad things from happening.

If the psychological pessimist like Jay beats his breast and laments, "I am worthless, life is hopeless and it's all my own damn fault," his religious pessimism takes the argument one step further to, "And God is going to get me for it. I'm doomed."[2]

---

[1] Our "explanatory style"—or how we explain setbacks to ourselves—is explored in the book *Learned Optimism*, by Martin E. P. Seligman, Ph.D., a psychologist at the University of Pennsylvania whose research forms the basis for the discussion of optimism and pessimism in this chapter.

[2] In *Guilt Is the Teacher, Love Is the Lesson* I called this line of thinking spiritual pessimism. I'm sorry that I did. More properly, I should have called it religious pessimism. While this kind of crime-and-punishment thinking occurs in many religious contexts, it does not, by definition, occur in a spiritual context. In order to understand why, consider this fine distinction between religion and spirituality made by psychotherapist Rachel Naomi Remen, M.D.: "The spiritual

Religions that lead us to experiences of interconnectedness and deep participation with one another and the divine are bridges to the spiritual. They direct us to that indwelling center—the Self—in which safety, communion, awe, gratitude, compassion, joy and wisdom are matters of experience rather than dogma. The core of all great religious traditions is essentially the same—to connect deeply and thankfully with life by loving ourselves, one another and God. Jesus summed up the teachings of Christianity as being the same as the primary teaching of the Pharisaic Judaism of his time: "Love the Lord your God with all your heart, with all your soul and with all your mind, and love your neighbor as yourself."

A problem arises in religious teachings, however, when fear is used in an attempt to inculcate love. This tactic is an obvious impossibility that defies common sense and defiles what it is to be loving. Hearkening back to our previous discussion of God as father, a parent who attempts to criticize and threaten a child into being polite, loving and respectful generally produces a helpless, ashamed and angry offspring. The child may put on a mask of niceness, politeness and piety, but underneath is a seething volcano of resentment, and guilt for feeling that way. If our secular psychology has figured out this much, it is a good bet that God knew it long ago.

Looking back to your own answer to the question "Why me?" are you a psychological pessimist like Jay who helplessly blames yourself for the problems of your life, or are you an optimist like Leslie who believes that life's challenges are part of your psychological and spiritual growth? Are you a religious pessimist or a spiritual optimist? Jay's pessimistic theory was that his illness was proof that he was a sinner destined for eternal punishment. Leslie's theory about her illness is much more benign. Her strength is in the admission "I don't know why these bad things happened," coupled with her faith

---

is not the religious. A religion is a dogma, a set of beliefs about the spiritual and a set of practices which rise out of those beliefs. There are many religions and they tend to be mutually exclusive. That is, every religion tends to think that it has dibs on the spiritual—that it's 'The Way.' Yet the spiritual is inclusive. It is the deepest sense of belonging and participation. . . . One might say that the spiritual is that realm of human experience which religion attempts to connect us to through dogma and practice. Sometimes it succeeds and sometimes it fails. *Religion is a bridge to the spiritual, but the spiritual lies beyond religion* [italics added]."

that the pain she experiences will someday be revealed as part of a
larger wholeness.

IS THE UNIVERSE A FRIENDLY PLACE
OR NOT?

Albert Einstein's view of life was similar to Leslie's. To Einstein
the universe was mysterious and magnificent, awesome and holy—
a "great eternal riddle" that is only partially knowable. The quantum
mechanical view of the universe that Einstein introduced in 1905
rocked the world of science. Instead of a machine-like universe where
separate factors operate by simple cause and effect, the quantum
mechanical revolution that Einstein began speaks to the notion that
all things are interrelated in one great field of energy. At some level,
everything is actually part of an interconnected Whole.

Einstein's genius for apprehending creation through mathematics
led him to the physical/mystical understanding that the idea that we
are separate entities is simply an "optical delusion of our consciousness." What, then, would Einstein have said in answer to the question
"Why me?" In his luminous book *Recovering the Soul,* physician
Larry Dossey relates that, during a serious illness, Einstein was asked
if he was afraid of death. He replied, "I feel such a sense of solidarity
with all living things that it does not matter to me where the individual begins and ends." Dossey continues,

> Where did the individual begin and end for Einstein? The
> boundaries of the person were seemingly far-flung. We get
> a hint of this view in his attitude about freedom of the will,
> in which he reveals his belief that we have unseverable ties
> with all the things and events of the world—an affinity
> which is so intimate that the entire question of individual
> freedom is nonsensical. Our concept of freedom of the will
> in one sense is very limited, implying an isolated individual
> situated in the here-and-now who can exercise it. Einstein
> does not share this local concept. For him, freedom of the

will is tied to an endless chain of events extending far into
the past in an indefinitely large expansion (p. 147).

To Einstein, Jay's notion that we are 100 percent responsible for
creating our own reality would have been too simpleminded. Who
is the "I" separate from the "we" who has the hubris to think that
it acts in isolation? Strangers wrote to Einstein from all over the
world about their hopes and dreams, their suffering and fears. At
one point Einstein was asked what he thought the most important
question was that a human being needed to answer. His reply was,
"Is the universe a friendly place or not?" And indeed, our answer
to that question is the cornerstone on which many of our values
and beliefs inevitably rest. If we believe that the universe is unfriendly and that our very souls are in danger, peace will be elusive
at best.

What is your answer to the question "Is the universe a friendly
place or not?" Hopefully, in returning our attention to the plight of
Job, you can think about your response to this critical question and
perhaps gain some new insights into your most basic beliefs.

IS THERE AN ANSWER FOR JOB?

The Book of Job goes on to provide considerable insight into how
people think about the question of whether the universe is a friendly
place or not. After Job's stirring soliloquy of suffering and misery
that we read a few pages back, his three friends sit with him in silence
for a week, pondering his situation. It is clear from the subsequent
conversation that Job's friends are absolutely terrified. After all, Job
is supposedly a just man, but he has been sorely afflicted. Why? What
are the implications of his suffering to their belief system?

In commentary that accompanies his translation of *The Book of
Job*, Stephen Mitchell points out that if Job is suffering even though
he is a righteous man, then the friends are left with only two conclusions. Either God is unjust (and the universe is therefore a very
unfriendly place) or suffering has nothing to do with whether or not

a person has sinned (the universe is also potentially unfriendly since anything can happen to anyone). The most popular explanation among the friends, and the only one in which their limited thinking perceives safety, is that Job is a sinner who is therefore being punished. As theologian Elaine Pagels points out in her book *Adam, Eve and the Serpent,* and as Jay demonstrated in his response to AIDS, most people prefer guilt to helplessness to the extent that it feels empowering. At least if something bad is happening it's your own fault; by extension, if you're really, really good, then bad things won't happen.

Since the belief that God is just and people suffer only when they sin is the explanation that superficially minimizes helplessness, Job's three friends take turns haranguing him and trying to get him to confess his sins. Eliphaz the Temanite speaks to Job of the harshness of God, the inevitability of human sin and the intrinsic worthlessness of human nature. Once again, the imagery of the Old Testament poet is strong and vivid: "*Can mortal man be righteous before God? Can a man be pure before his maker? Even in his servants he puts no trust, and his angels he charges with error.*" Bildad the Shuhite continues to discourse on the inevitable wages of sin: "*Yea, the light of the wicked is put out. . . . Terrors frighten him on every side, and chase him at his heels. . . . His roots dry up beneath, and his branches wither above.*"

Job, however, is having none of this. He knows that he hasn't sinned and is thus confronted with the unsavory possibility that there is no justice based on righteousness: "*Though I am blameless, he would prove me perverse. . . . therefore I say, he destroys both the blameless and the wicked. When disaster brings sudden death, he mocks at the calamity of the innocent.*"

Then, much to Job's astonishment, God speaks to him from a whirlwind and asks, "*Who is this that darkens counsel by words without knowledge? . . . Where were you when I laid the foundation of the earth?*" Job's ego is getting its comeuppance. What hubris to think we can know the divine plan and, with our limited sight that sees "but through a glass darkly," as the Apostle Paul put it, create a blueprint for God to obey.

God goes on to enumerate all his powers and to speak of both the majesty and terror of nature at great length. Job is essentially speechless, and we are left to imagine how he was affected by this powerful meeting, based on the strength of just a few lines that he utters in response to God. His simple comment, *"Therefore I have uttered what I did not understand, things too wonderful for me, which I did not know,"* says volumes about how it is impossible to comprehend the infinite with a finite mind.

Job's last words to God in standard translations of the parable are *"I had heard of thee by hearing of the ear, but now my eye sees thee, therefore I despise myself, and repent in dust and ashes."* Mitchell, in stark contrast, comments that the verb that has been translated "despise" actually means "reject" or "regard as of little value." Furthermore, the object of the verb is not "myself." Mitchell proposes that a sounder interpretation, first suggested in an ancient Syriac translation, would be: "Therefore I take back (everything I said.)" As for repenting in dust and ashes, Mitchell's interpretation of Job's last words have to do instead with comfort in his mortality.

"I had heard of thee by the hearing of the ear, but now my eye sees thee; therefore I take back everything I said, comforted that I am dust" suggests that the wonderful new understanding of which Job previously spoke has revised his previous ideas about God. The standard translators, however, rather than being true to the Hebrew text, rendered Job's last words in line with the religiously pessimistic preconceptions of orthodox Christianity. This viewpoint holds that self-deprecation, guilt and shame are the appropriate responses to avert the wrath of the righteous, ill-tempered Jehovah.

Groveling in submission before the hideous power of the Almighty, a kind of "Yes, Boss, I'll do anything—just lay off" mentality, would be an anticlimactic end to the power of this poetic First Story. Mitchell has a different interpretation:

> When Job says, "I had heard of you with my ears; but now I have seen you," he is no longer a servant, who fears god and avoids evil. He has faced evil, has looked straight into its face and through it, into a vast wonder of love . . . . Job's

comfort at the end is in his mortality. The physical body is acknowledged as dust, the personal drama as delusion. It is as if the world we perceive through our senses, that whole gorgeous and terrible pageant, were the breath-thin surface of a bubble, and everything else, inside and outside, is pure radiance. Both suffering and joy come then like a brief reflection, and death like a pin (pp. xxvii–xxviii).

YOUR OWN ANSWER TO JOB

Through the years I have had the opportunity to talk with dozens of near-death experiencers who, like Job, have found comfort in their mortality. After returning from clinical death, these people—whether Jews, Christians, atheists or agnostics—have described the experience of dying as "like taking off a heavy suit of clothes," "waking up from a dream," "encountering indescribable radiance and bliss," "being connected with all things," "having total knowledge," "seeing how every event in my life made complete sense."

I believe that the First Story of Job is an invitation to come face to face with our own ideas about suffering and death, and, like Job, to see God with new eyes. Do we suffer even though God is loving, as Rabbi Harold Kushner suggests, because the universe is still incompletely formed and pockets of chaos exist in which bad things happen to good people? Or is the universe a perfectly ordered freedom play in which there are no accidents? Do we suffer because an authoritarian father God punishes us for our sins, or because we are the helpless/hapless authors of our own fate?

If, like Job, we plumb the depths of our dark nights and catch a true glimpse of the divine, perhaps we will indeed be comforted that we are dust. The drama of this body we hold so dear may then appear to be but one act in a cosmic play of epic proportions. Transformed by the eternal radiance in whose stories we grow and ripen, perhaps we might then accept our suffering as the seeds of an awakening.

I hope that in the course of the chapters that follow, the way in which you have added your own stories about suffering to God's, and come closer to or moved further from that radiance, will become evident. For if we are willing to give up our stories of fear and gaze with new eyes into the face of love, perhaps someday we will find a new meaning in our suffering and, as Kahlil Gibran promises in *The Prophet,* "come to bless the darkness as we have blessed the light."

CHAPTER TWO

The Search for Meaning

Man's main concern is not to gain pleasure or to avoid pain but rather to see a meaning in his life. That is why man is even ready to suffer, on the condition, to be sure, that his suffering has a meaning.

Viktor Frankl

I was sitting in the dining room several weeks after my son's friend Mat Hitchcock died, looking out through a big picture window. Beds of petunias and cosmos, flowering and producing seed in their short season, blazed in pink and purple splendor in our quiet yard. The sweet scent of honeysuckle wafted in through the screen and I sat in a kind of reverie, thinking about how life had changed in the month since Mat's death.

Mat's mother, Yvonne Drew, and I had bonded through the tragedy, and our friendship was growing. My husband, Myrin, and I had likewise become closer to several of Andrei's friends who, prior to the tragedy, had moved through the house with relative anonymity, stopping to chat about "safe" things, impersonal things like the weather or the color of their new sneakers. I was reflecting on what one of them had pointed out—that it was too bad tragedy had to strike for people to slow down and show their real selves to one another.

Life did indeed seem curiously fuller since Mat's death. I was thinking about how his loss had woven lives together in a way that never would have happened otherwise and how he would have liked that. I was missing him, too, tears welling up as I thought about his family's loss, our family's loss and, to some extent, all the losses we suffer in life. The doorbell interrupted my reverie. It was the agent of Providence, the anonymous hand of coincidence, disguised as a UPS delivery man.

He plunked down two big boxes. Andrei knew what they were right away. They were copies of the "Mat book," compiled from pages that his friends and family had written in the days following his death. Andrei was too excited to go into the kitchen for a knife. He tore the packing tape off with his bare hands. The colorful cover of the top copy nearly jumped out of the crate. It was a flaming heart, drawn by one of Mat's friends. The kids had decided on the cover two days after Mat's accident, the night that almost fifty of them had gathered at our home to write a page for the book.

After his family had received it and added their own pages, we had intended to take the book to a local printer so that every person who had written a page could have a copy of the whole book. Mat's father, however, is an artist and volunteered to have the book laid out and printed more professionally. I was wondering if he would give the book a title. He had. And it addressed the question of why bad things happen very simply. The title was *Love Is the Answer*.

"Love is the answer" is a radical statement that may appear simplistic, maudlin, foolish or a wishful cover-up for grief. My conventional training in psychology would write off such a statement as "magical thinking," out of touch with reality. But what is the reality we are out of touch with? According to conventional scientific thinking, reality is that which is directly observable and measurable. In a world that is clearly unsafe, where seventeen-year-olds die in car accidents and leave their loved ones heartbroken, "Love is the answer" seems illogical. But, according to the experience of more than thirteen million Americans (the 5 percent of us who have survived clinical death and returned to tell others about the near-death experience), it is science that is out of touch with a larger reality where love is, indeed, the very fabric of existence.

WHISPERS OF ETERNITY—
EVIDENCE FOR A LARGER REALITY

While there are many worldviews that claim to describe reality—scientific, psychological and religious—they lack impact unless they accurately describe human experience. When journalist Bill Moyers asked mythologist Joseph Campbell whether he was a man of faith, Campbell laughed and explained that he didn't need faith because he had experience. Although people have always had experiences that defy our usual beliefs about life, until recently these experiences have remained outside mainstream awareness.

As a medical psychologist I have heard dozens of stories that defy conventional scientific and psychological theory. In *Guilt Is the Teacher, Love Is the Lesson* I told several stories of patients, colleagues and friends who had visions, near-death experiences and meetings with a radiant light through which they directly apprehended higher levels of meaning, found physical and/or psychological healing and came to believe, like Mat's father, that despite the tragedies and trials of life they were safe in a universe that was ultimately loving.

"David," for example, had recently discovered that he was an incest survivor. Shocking, painful memories of his father's betrayal that surfaced for the first time at age forty-one made it hard for him to function, a common occurrence when repressed trauma comes to light. What was unusual about David is that he became aware of a loving, protective—in his words, "angelic"—presence that provided information about his father's childhood that helped explain why he had grown up abusive. David felt safe and cared for by the unseen presence.

The feeling of safety—and the strong belief in a loving universe that it awakened—allowed David to move very quickly through the stages of recovery from incest. In a relatively short time he was able to grieve his childhood, access the anger toward his father, understand the origin of the abuse in his father's own childhood pain and then forgive both his father and himself. David also came to peace with the fact that his father was unlikely to take responsibility for his actions and that it was best not to see him again, at least in the forseeable future.

When David tried to tell his therapist about the angelic presence, however, his experience was dismissed as "magical thinking," and he wisely decided to keep that aspect of his healing out of the therapy. Science has declared such experiences impossible, and psychology has sought to explain them away as episodes of mental illness. As Lily Tomlin once quipped, "When we speak to God we are said to be praying, but when God speaks to us we are said to be schizophrenic!"

Data from studies conducted by the National Social Survey based at the University of Chicago indicate just the opposite. People who have direct experiences of the sacred score at the top of the scale for mental health. Visionary experiences are not the province of mentally ill people or misinformed, fanatical weirdos. Furthermore, they are not rare. Fully 35 percent of the American people have actually seen a vision—a dead relative, an angel, an apparition of light, an entire scene from another level of reality. Fearful of ridicule, a majority of these people keep their experiences to themselves, a fact that is beginning to change as we let our mysticism out of the closet.

The general public is currently far more accepting of these experiences than my psychological and scientific colleagues are. Since visions and voices can also be symptoms of psychosis, in which a person is unable to separate everyday reality from hallucinations, there is certainly reason for caution. Visionary experiences, however, are quite different from psychotic hallucinations. Whereas psychosis usually leads to losing touch with this reality (not being able to tell what is real and what is imagined) and to dysfunctional behavior, transcendent visions lead to an expanded appreciation of this reality and to more adaptive, healthy behavior.

Modern-day science denies visions, angels, near-death experiences and the central observation of human beings from every culture that "mind" or consciousness seems to exist beyond the localized limits of the brain. Knowing who will be on the other end of a ringing telephone, an impulse to turn around in your car because you sense that someone in another car is staring at you and precognitive dreams are common experiences that challenge the localization of mind to the brain and suggest that it might instead extend through space. Growing popular interest in these experiences of what Larry Dossey, M.D., calls "nonlocal mind" is challenging members of the scientific and psychological communities to question their most cherished beliefs.

During visionary experiences, people report that they are in connection with a wisdom that transcends our ordinary perception of life and makes sense of the apparently senseless world in which we live. Following such experiences people are often left with an abiding sense of love, security and faith in the ultimate friendliness of the universe. David, for example, not only healed from the incest experience but came to view it as an unpleasant but necessary step in the unfolding of his own life purpose as a therapist who remains intimately connected to the wisdom and guidance of the "unseen" world.

Raymond Moody, M.D., is a physician who is a serious student of the unseen world and the benevolent guides, angels or beings of light that so many people have reported to him as part of near-death experiences (NDEs). In *The Light Beyond,* Moody discusses the remarkable meetings with these beings that people of different belief systems—scientists, psychologists, Christians, Jews, atheists and others—report after they have been revived from clinical death. Once people move through the tunnel often described in association with these experiences, they meet beings of light that "glow with a beautiful and intense luminescence that seems to permeate everything and fill the person with love."

Following meetings with different light beings who act as guides, the NDE experiencer usually meets what Moody calls a Supreme Being of Light. The description of this being varies with the religious orientation of the dying person. We seem to experience God, to some extent, through the filter of our own beliefs. Some describe the Supreme Being of Light as Jesus or a father God of consummate love and forgiveness. Others are awed by the holiness but attach no specific religious or cultural identity to this Supreme Being.

When I lecture about near-death experiences, people often come up to me afterward to share their own NDE or to put me in contact with others who have had such experiences. One of the most fascinating accounts I have heard was that of Donna J. Elsten who kept detailed notes of two NDEs she had in her thirties, both of which happened when her heart stopped during surgery. She has generously made these accounts available for us to read.

In her second NDE, Donna describes leaving her body, looking down at the operating room scene, hearing the medical staff yelling that they'd "lost her" and then floating off into a "bold, bright, white light." She then moves through a tunnel that she describes in great detail, feeling peaceful, calmer and more loving as she ascends through it. She notes,

> I am slowly, slowly floating and floating. I love, love, love. I love myself. I am filled with love. I am experiencing affection on an immeasurable level. This affection and love is sent to me and is coming from me to me at me at the same time. The affection I feel in me is for everything, not just myself. I understand this. . . . I feel the deepest feeling of acceptance. I am loved. It is beautiful here. It is so peaceful. It is so tranquil. . . . The weight of life is lifted off my shoulders.

As Donna continues to float into the light, the feelings of love intensify until, midway through the tunnel, she meets a Supreme Being of Light:

> I know this is God. As we come face to face nothing is said. God makes the gesture—holding His hand out. . . . The touch is a connected bond, an immeasurable emotional and intellectual bond. . . . I am gifted with an immeasurable capacity for grasping knowledge and understanding. This ability is beyond any earthly ability. Instantly I am aware of His power. He is the Source of all things. . . . He is a truly forgiving God. . . . He is capable of forgiving everyone for everything and He does forgive. God telepathically tells me why He is so forgiving. They don't know any better is why He forgives.

Donna's glimpse into an expanded reality continues to unfold as she experiences eternity:

> Here where the light is time doesn't pass. Time stops. There is no time. I experience eternity. This endless existence is

inconceivable on earth. No end to existence. Our life on earth is like a flash of lightning. We come down and in a flash our earthly lives are over. Our stay on earth is so short. A snap of my fingers and this measures the time spent on earth. I'm no longer a prisoner of death. There is no death here. Death doesn't exist. I'm not afraid of death. Through this soul somehow, I see the miracles of life. How precious life is. How it is to be treasured. I love life. I appreciate every life. Everything.

When Donna was finally revived after great difficulty, she left the state of eternity and returned to her body and the everyday experience of time. But the deep appreciation and reverence for life that she described during her "glimpse into eternity" remained with her. This expansive gratitude and respect for life is a common feature of NDEs. Like the Native Americans, people who have had NDEs experience that we are part of the earth and the earth is part of us. We cannot hurt any living thing without hurting ourselves, nor can we nurture anything or anyone without also nurturing ourselves.

The emotional interconnectedness of our lives is made particularly clear by studying the experiences of those people who undergo a life review as part of their NDE. According to polls taken by George Gallup, Jr., 32 percent of people who have NDEs report a life review. Like Donna, they experience a Supreme Being of Light who is totally loving and forgiving. In that divine presence they observe their lives in a complete panorama, as if all the events were happening simultaneously.

When their actions in life caused pain, they feel that pain. When their actions extended love, they feel that love. With the help of the Supreme Being of Light, they are able to put the events of their life into perspective. Telepathically they make sense of their experience and ascertain how loving they were—the yardstick of a life well lived. When such people return to their bodies, the overwhelming majority believe that the most important thing in life is love. For most, the second most important thing is knowledge. Love and knowledge, they tell us, are the only two things we take with us when we die.

Coming back to the physical body after a near-death experience is usually a reluctant choice because it requires temporarily relinquishing the state of perfect love and forgetting the transcendent wisdom that makes sense of the difficulties we inevitably experience while in the body. When I have interviewed survivors of clinical death and asked why they chose to return, the answer almost always concerns continuing specific loving relationships with other people—often small children they wish to care for—or learning more about love in general.

One woman reported asking one of her guides in the life review what she would gain from the choice to return—"Why would I want to live in a body? Earth is a place filled with pain, suffering, loss and disappointment. Why would anyone want to be there when they could be here?" The Being of Light explained that life on earth, precisely because of the suffering, is the finest opportunity to learn about love. From this perspective, Mat Hitchcock's father chose a most fitting title for the book saluting his son's short life: *Love Is the Answer*.

BELIEFS THAT LIMIT THE ABILITY TO GROW FROM CRISIS

When tragedy, illness or misfortune occur, it is human nature to question our belief systems. Although questioning is healthy in the long run, in the short run it can be extremely painful, leading to a "crisis in faith" in which previous comforting beliefs drop away and leave us feeling temporarily vulnerable. The AIDS patient Jay, whom you met in the last chapter, had several crises of faith. He doubted the agnosticism he believed in prior to being diagnosed with AIDS, and, in compensation, he resubscribed to the fire-and-brimstone, "God is punishing me" beliefs of his childhood. When those beliefs seemed more frightening than comforting he jumped on the seemingly empowering New Age "you create your entire reality" bandwagon and hoped to think himself well. When that belief system crumbled he was left in a panic.

The difficulty Jay experienced in finding growth and meaning in living with AIDS came from his desire to know absolutely and for certain what the AIDS meant. In other words, he got stuck in trying to figure out whether he was responsible for (translate this as "guilty for") getting sick, rather than asking the more meaningful question often posed by the Buddhist teacher and therapist Stephen Levine, "What does it mean to be responsible *to* my illness?"

Family therapist John Bradshaw defines responsible as "response able"—able to pay attention to and respond to the events of life. In my experience, those people who are able to find a meaning in their illness or tragedy focus on being responsible to the situation by using it as an occasion to attain greater freedom and happiness, rather than seeking theological knowledge about why bad things happen.

You may remember that Leslie, whom you also met in the last chapter, dealt with the death of her husband and her own cancer with a "don't know why" attitude that was based on the underlying premise that our spiritual sight is too narrow to really apprehend the meaning of tragedy, although she believed that a loving purpose would be revealed at some future time. In the meantime, her intent was to be responsible to her life—to seek good health by caring for body and mind, to focus on loving relationships and to stay open to what the future might bring, even though she was sometimes afraid. Leslie's faith was flexible, open and based on living with love. Jay's faith was rigid, closed and focused on avoiding punishment and fear.

Perhaps you can relate to the following example of rigid faith and how it can block new understanding. I gave a talk once in southern Texas, deep in the heart of the Bible Belt. At the intermission a man approached me, red-faced and angry. He described himself as a Christian counselor and accused me of being an irresponsible "New-Ager." I tried to explain that I was more of an "Old-Ager," attempting to unite the most ancient traditions of wisdom—Jewish, Christian, Native American, Goddess-centered and Eastern—with what we were now learning scientifically and psychologically. That didn't satisfy him one bit. Teeth clenched and arms crossed, he moved in for the kill. "Just tell me," he gloated, "do you believe in creation or do you believe in evolution?"

My reply was that I saw no contradiction between evolution and creation. For a higher consciousness to create a universe that keeps expanding seems the height of elegance to me. Why separate God from her creation? (I like to think about the creative aspect of divinity as a feminine attribute of a Whole that is ultimately beyond gender). Apparently my answer was not satisfactory, so the man left. My point of view was a threat to his belief that the entire world literally had been created in six calendar days.

To this counselor, life was a sometimes unpleasant stopover on the way to an eternity in purgatory, hell or a heaven that only a few good Christians ever got to. He was particularly angered by my remark that of the thousands of accounts of people who have had an NDE—including convicted criminals—only one that I knew of had been at all negative. All the others, regardless of the religious beliefs of the resuscitated person, spoke of a loving, benevolent, forgiving God. These testimonies were threatening to the counselor because they called his beliefs about eternal punishment in Hell into question.

The counselor's belief system—that only God-fearing Christians get "saved"—was a good example of what theologian and researcher Dr. James Fowler has termed Stage-Two Faith—a concrete and literal theology. In *Stages of Faith: The Psychology of Human Development and the Quest for Meaning*, Fowler outlines six phases in the development of faith that parallel our psychological development through childhood to fully functioning, loving adulthood. It is important to realize that we can get stuck at any of these stages. Although we may be thirty or forty or sixty or eighty, there is an inner child within each of us who is still looking for unconditional love and protecting itself from rejection and pain. If that child is unhealed, it recreates past pain, contaminating our adult thoughts, feelings and relationships. According to Fowler's model, it also contaminates our beliefs about God.

THE STAGES OF FAITH

The six stages Fowler outlines in the development of faith, modified somewhat by my own understanding, are:

1. **Intuitive-projective faith.** This stage is typical of young children who hear stories about God and weave these into vivid imaginings of heaven and love, on the one hand, or a fiery hell full of demons, on

the other. The gift of this stage is the ability to experience the world in powerful images that remain in the unconscious for a lifetime. The danger of this stage is in what Fowler calls the "possession of the child's imagination by unrestrained images of terror and destructiveness." In this stage the foundation is set for how we perceive God's First Stories, and whether we add chapters of love to them or bury them in fear.

2. **Mythic-literal faith.** In school-aged children imagination declines and the literal, uncompromising acceptance of symbols, rules and morals takes over. This worldview revolves around fairness, reward and retribution. Biblical stories are taken literally, without the capacity to "step back from the flow of stories to formulate reflective, conceptual meanings." This is the eye-for-an-eye and tooth-for-a-tooth level that informed the faith of both Jay and the Christian counselor.

3. **Synthetic-conventional faith.** The advent of puberty brings with it the capacity to look beyond one's family of origin (and the dogma and doctrine of one's childhood religion) and to synthesize one's expanding knowledge of the world in a way that provides a stable base for future experience. In other words, at this stage we begin to develop the capacity to think for ourselves. But although we have a personal ideology, we have not yet stepped back to examine it systematically. It hasn't been tested. The various losses and tragedies of life are catalysts for such testing that move us along to the next stage.

4. **Individuative-reflective faith.** The older adolescent begins to take responsibility for his or her beliefs and actions. The self-reflective capacity that develops at this time leads to a reevaluation of faith that Fowler suggests may be triggered by the breakthrough of childhood images, by a voice from the inner self, by the perceived emptiness or irrelevance of previous beliefs, or by an attraction to the stories, symbols and myths of other religions or cultures.

In my estimation, the conscious mind of the adolescent is ready to entertain the archetypal First Stories that live eternally in the Great Unconscious—the imaginal realm that we will discuss in later

chapters—and that presage a life of adventure and awakening. Epic
stories like *E.T.* and *Star Wars* are often pivotal in opening the
adolescent mind to a reconsideration of life's meaning.

5. **Conjunctive faith.** Fowler states that Stage Five, which often occurs in mid-life, "knows the sacrament of defeat." A lot of living has
gone on in the years between late adolescence and mid-life, living
that has repeatedly called our faith into question and pointed out the
scarcity of answers we have to the big questions like "Who am I?"
and "What is life all about?" Whereas previous stages revolved around
figuring out the boundaries of things, this stage thrives on paradox
and an openness to the truths of those who would previously have
been thought of as "other." Myths and symbols are grasped at a deeper
level, and we have the chance to integrate parts of our experience that
were previously denied because they didn't fit in with our beliefs.

6. **Universalizing faith.** At this stage, which I believe more and more
people are operating out of, we act on the knowledge that divisions
between people must be overcome and that compassion is the fullest
expression of faith. Fowler cites Gandhi, Martin Luther King in the
last years of his life, Mother Teresa, Dag Hammarskjöld, Dietrich
Bonhoeffer, Abraham Heschel and Thomas Merton as examples of
universalizing faith. Stage Six doesn't mean perfection or self-actualization. Instead it refers to a practical commitment, in Fowler's
terms, to "making the Kingdom actual," bringing into being a world
based on connectedness, understanding, wise use of resources and
kindness.

If all goes well, and we heal ourselves from the childhood wounds
that may keep us stuck at one stage or another, we progress through
these six stages in the course of a lifetime. In discussing movement
from a literal, concrete stage of faith to a more universal faith in
which metaphor and personal experience inform a broader understanding, Fowler observes that "a factor initiating transition . . . is
the implicit clash or contradiction in stories that leads to reflection
on meanings. . . . Previous literalism breaks down . . . [and] leads

to disillusionment with previous teachers and teachings. Conflicts between authoritative stories (Genesis on creation versus evolutionary theory) must be faced."

Fowler described the Christian counselor's faith as Stage Two and helped me realize that it is fruitless to have theological discussions with people at this mythic-literal stage because it is too psychologically threatening for them. Tragedy, however, can break through literalism and, painful though it is, lead to a healing of the wounds of childhood that can, in turn, inform an expanded faith. This is what the phenomenon of "hitting bottom" is about. We can go on living life with the wounds and beliefs of childhood even though we may feel chronically empty or unhappy. But when crisis strikes—whether it's cancer or an arrest for drunk driving—we are called to be responsible to the tragedy. In the process our beliefs may change quite radically.

EXITING THE CAVE OF OLD BELIEFS

Physician Larry Dossey tells the story of Charles Darwin's landing in Micronesia. The natives there had no concept of what a large, oceangoing ship was. Accustomed to staying in the vicinity of their own islands, these people had only small boats. They had no imagination of or language for anything bigger. Darwin and his crew arrived in the *Beagle*, a large vessel. Although the natives saw them coming ashore in their small landing boats, when the *Beagle* was pointed out to them they literally could not see it. It was invisible to minds that believed such a big ship to be impossible.

Plato spoke to the relative inability of people to take in information outside their usual belief systems in his enduring classic *The Republic*. He related a parable of a people who lived in chains, facing the back wall of a dark cave. The only reality they knew consisted of shadows cast by the activity from the outside world. Finally, one of them became bold enough to try to escape. He returned to set the people in the cave free from the prison of their illusions, reporting on a miraculous outside world of light, color and substance. The others could not believe him. They thought he was crazy because the new information could not be integrated into their previous experience.

My mother was like one of Plato's cave dwellers until the last few months of her life. While I grew up questioning life at every turn, searching for meaning, she would respond in all seriousness with the motto "Ignorance is bliss." When, at fifteen, I came home with information on the Unitarian Church, she put her foot down. Although she wasn't a believing Jew, she felt that religious questing could only lead to psychic upset at best and fanaticism at worst. In a similar vein, she believed that questioning your feelings and experiences of life could also be upsetting. Tossing my Unitarian literature in the trash, she issued a clear directive: "I forbid you to read about any other religions or to study psychology. I say this for your own good!"

Since I grew up to be a scientist and psychologist with a major interest in religion and philosophy, I can truly say that I owe my mother all that I am. She was the perfect foil for a rebellious nature and I am grateful to her. She played her part in the drama of my life perfectly, contributing the precise energy required to spur the quest for meaning! In the thirty years that have passed since her encyclical barring psychospiritual exploration, the quest for psychological and religious understanding has become a popular one, a search whose value even she accepted in the final year of her life.

The event that triggered her awakening was a remarkable one. Mom was an avid baseball fan. In 1988 a player for the Boston Red Sox, Wade Boggs, became the subject of a national scandal when an affair he was having became fodder for the media gossip mill. The *Boston Globe* published an interview with Boggs, focusing on why he seemed to be able to handle the charges and the continuing sordid revelations with such equanimity. Boggs attributed his peacefulness to advice from his mother, who had recently died. According to his account, the spirit of his mother had appeared in a vision to his sister, whose vocal cords were paralyzed from multiple sclerosis, and asked her to speak at the funeral. Miraculously, the sister was able to do so. Their mother also appeared to Boggs, reassuring him that everything would be all right, that he needn't worry.

Whereas the conversations that Mom and I had about the continuity of the spirit after bodily death had left her unmoved, the story of Wade Boggs's mother spoke to her. It brought about a fundamental change in her beliefs, and she showed great peace and courage while facing the final months of a debilitating illness. When she was admitted to the hospital for the last time, close to death, a nurse held her hand in the emergency room. "Mrs. Zakon," she said with compassion, "the end of life is near. Have you made your peace? Have you thought about death?" My mother rallied from her stupor like a missionary: "I know all about it. I'm ready. Have you heard about Wade Boggs's mother?" To the complete surprise of the gentle nurse, her patient fairly resurrected from death's door to report on the latest version of the "good news"!

The events that call us forth from Plato's cave are different for each person. For my own family, the death of young Mathew Hitchcock was one such event. Our son Andrei responded to Mat's death with a deep sorrow that ripened into an increased gratitude for life and a powerful realization that loving relationships are the most precious thing we can aspire to. Andrei is well aware of the gifts he received both through Mat's loving friendship and also through his death. "Perhaps the Native Americans are right," Andrei said of Mat's death, "when they say that every human and animal is born with a certain number of days to their circle. Some lives are long and others are short, but each one is complete."

We like to think that Mat lived the full circle of his life in seventeen years, and we believe that his life continues not only in other realms, but also in this one. We drop like pebbles into the ponds of each other's souls, and the orbit of our ripples continues to expand, intersecting with countless others. Mat's ripples will continue to spread his joyfulness, humility, creativity, caring and love through all the people who were privileged to know him. For, in order for our suffering to have any meaning at all, it must ultimately increase the capacity of all humankind both to love and to be loved.

CHAPTER THREE
Crisis as Initiation

One thing that comes out in myths is that at the bottom of the abyss comes the voice of salvation. The black moment is the moment when the real message of transformation is going to come. At the darkest moment comes the light.

Joseph Campbell

I can vividly recall waiting for my son Justin's birth. Excitement and wonder continued to mount through the first part of labor on a snowy February day in Boston. I was more or less in control—breathing, counting, resting, waiting for the next contraction. Then transition struck. Transition marks the end of early labor and heralds what is referred to in an understated manner as "hard" labor. For me transition was a rite of passage, a dark night, a test of faith, a seemingly uncontrollable descent into an alien landscape of pain, Lamaze breathing notwithstanding. I felt certain that my body was being torn apart and that I would never survive the birth. I remember thinking that if the Universe offered me the chance to call the whole thing off right then and there, I would do so, no questions asked. No baby? No problem, no hard feelings. I would just pick up my things and go home.

Fortunately, the Universe made no such offer and I endured to witness the miracle of birth some thirty or forty interminable minutes later. I was enraptured not only by the tiny, perfect infant born wrapped in the cawl (the amnionic membranes) but by his umbilical cord. An iridescent pink and blue, it seemed to shine with an inner light. The otherworldy colors reflected its function of carrying red nutrient and oxygen-filled blood to the child, and returning the bluish, depleted blood to the mother for cleansing and recharging with life. As Justin was freed from the cawl and began to cry, having completed his own transition from the watery, dark world of the womb to the light of the world, the cord ceased to throb with life and he was on his own.

Two new people were born in that moment. Justin was born newly into this world and I was reborn, one of the many rebirths each of us experiences in the course of a lifetime. In the agonizing time of transition, when I had been left seemingly unsupported by the universe to traverse an unknown passage alone, a remarkable transformation occurred. Gone was the self-centered twenty-three-year-old student, more still a girl than a woman. I had labored to bring a child into the world, and the fear and pain I suffered had somehow awakened a new compassion in my heart. I could never more return to my pretransition existence, for I had been born into motherhood and must now be initiated into the mysteries of womanhood—the nourishing of life.

In some European cultures there is an old custom of burying the umbilical cord with the seed of a fruit. If all goes well, the little seed swells with water in the dark womb of the earth, splits open and dies. The dying seed gives birth to a growing shoot which, in five or six seasons, will mature into a tree that bears fruit in its turn. The tree and its fruit are the exclusive property of the child on whose umbilicus the growing tree has fed. In watching the tree die back in winter and reawaken in spring, the child is brought close to the mystery of the seasons and their metaphor for the births, deaths and transformations that are equally a part of human life. What child has not looked on with wonder as a seed sprouts, a plant or flower forms, and life is reborn anew?

While the metaphor is poetic and easy to appreciate, it is hard to apply to our own lives, which are a series of little deaths, a letting-go of the old to make room for something new to be born. Each of these letting-goes entails a transition—a passage—from the way things were to the way things will be. While we know what was and can often dream of what the future might hold, the period of passage is a kind of no-man's land, a limbo, a space that cannot always be defined.

Some of these passages are short, like the transition phase of labor. Others are long, like adolescence. Birth, puberty, childhood's end, marriage, old age, death—these are commonplace, expected, sometimes joyful and sometimes painful transitions. Illness, madness, loss, war, addiction—these are also commonplace but dreaded transitions that issue compelling invitations to become something new, something other than the self we were. The birth and characteristics of the new self are determined in large part by the stories we tell ourselves about why the time of darkness has come.

RETHINKING THE PASSAGE THROUGH DARKNESS

When I was about eight, my father was robbed at gunpoint in his store. I still remember the night he came home, white-faced and shaken. Although he was usually home by six o'clock, we didn't hear his key in the lock until nearly eight. He stood in the hall, hat in hand, and announced in a small voice that he had been held up. At first my mother and I misunderstood. We thought he had been detained by something. "No," he went on, "I mean held up at gunpoint."

He told us that his clerk "Red" took the robbery in stride. He even refused to give the thief his wallet, handing over his money but keeping his license and billfold. Dad, on the other hand, was terrified. He was never quite the same after that night. From an outgoing, upbeat man, at least on the surface, he became withdrawn and fearful. A few months after the incident my mother sat me down for a talk and told me that my father was having a "nervous breakdown." Over time my father gradually recovered, but the trauma was never fully healed.

Back in the early 1950s, when the robbery occurred, there was no cultural support for thinking of traumatic experiences as passages of rebirth that might lead to a deeper healing. But times are slowly changing. The tremendous success of the public television series in which Bill Moyers interviewed mythologist Joseph Campbell is based on our hunger for new meanings, particularly for a way to understand suffering. Campbell was adept in his ability to tell archetypal First Stories from different cultures in which the heroes and heroines faced seemingly endless and insurmountable terrors and trials on their way to attaining the gifts of wisdom.

This mythological approach to our stories of pain provides a larger context for personal growth than do traditional medical-psychological understandings. Dark nights of the soul—fear, depression, madness, trauma—are too often seen through the limiting lens of fear. In fear, we wish only to rid ourselves of apparent negativity rather than searching our souls for its gifts. Fear demands that the problem be fixed immediately by drugs or therapy so that the person can be restored to his original "normal" state.

Sigmund Freud likewise believed that when a person was cured of neurosis the best outcome that could be expected was return "to an ordinary state of unhappiness." But some mental health professionals believe, as I do, that many dark nights of the soul are initiations into a new way of being. If the patient is willing to respond to the darkness, then an exciting, life-affirming newness can often emerge. Often, however, we must hold onto the First Stories of suffering as a passage to wisdom even when the mental health professionals that are a needed part of our passage hold onto their own stories of fear.

A friend of mine, for example, was stricken with episodes of severe, recurrent depression. Fortunately, he had an excellent team of psychiatrists who conducted appropriate drug therapy and psychotherapy. Unfortunately, they were unwilling to support him in viewing the illness in a larger perspective. When he would discuss depression and hospitalization as rites of passage, as initiations that he felt would be ultimately strengthening psychologically and spiritually, his doctors tried to convince him that he was crazy. His very belief that the illness was a positive passage, even a "grace," was an indication to the psychiatrists of mental instability. Fortunately, my friend was able to profit from their care while at the same time holding onto the greater vision that the depression had a positive meaning.

If we have lost our cultural understanding of the value of darkness, we have also lost the priesthood whose function it was to bring us through these transitions. All too often our religious priesthood is as out of touch with sources of wisdom as is our secular priesthood, therapists and psychiatrists who think more in terms of pathology than they do of growth and potential. We can learn a great deal about approaching these times of transition by observing how the priesthood of more "primitive" societies treats people in transition, whether the transition comes unbidden or is set into motion by a special ritual of passage.

THE DWELLER AT THE THRESHOLD

Anthropologist Victor Turner is well known for his study of the ritual process in different cultures, and it is from his research and writings that my comments about ritual are drawn. A ritual is a rite of passage, a transition between two distinct states of being or stations in society. The traditional rite of passage in "primitive" cultures consists of three distinct stages: the *separation* from one's previous state of being; the *liminal period,* during which one dwells between two worlds, not-here and not-there; and the *reincorporation* into some new role or status in the society. The ambiguous, intermediate state of liminality is often compared to being in the womb, in a state of darkness and invisibility or wandering in the wilderness.

Turner spent considerable time in Zambia, a country in south-central Africa, studying ritual in the Ndembu tribe. Whether the ritual was the installation of a new chief, puberty or marriage, the rite of passage always comprised the stages of separation, liminality and reincorporation. Separated from the tribe, the initiate no longer had his or her usual routine to define role, behavior or self-image. On the threshold of a new role, vestiges of the old self that might interfere with the new station were cleansed away. The initiate was often scourged physically or mentally. Chastisement, humiliation and physical deprivation were characteristic of this period. The liminal person owned nothing. Everything had been taken away as part of a symbolic return to a state of humility and innocence, like unworked clay suitable to be molded into a new form.

The collective hypnosis, our unconscious adherence to the familiar beliefs that guide our lives, is broken in the liminal period. In exactly the same way, our own uncelebrated life crises strip us of what we think we know, delivering us to the threshold of the unknown. In times of transition we awaken from the familiar trance of life and find ourselves in alien territory. If we knew that this frightening, unknown period was a necessary transition—like the transition period of labor—we could more easily ask for whatever help was needed and more patiently hold on and wait for the birth. We could take comfort that the process was natural, not pathological.

Each dark night and little death peels away a layer of conditioning, restoring our sight so that we can apprehend reality more clearly. Writing about male puberty rites in *Forest of Symbols: Aspects of Ndembu Ritual,* Turner states:

> As members of society, most of us see only what we expect to see, and what we expect to see is what we are conditioned to see when we have learned the definitions and classifications of our culture. A society's secular definitions do not allow for the existence of a not-boy-not-man, which is what a novice in a male puberty rite is (if he can be said to be anything). A set of essentially religious definitions co-exist with these which do set out to define the structurally indefinable "transitional-being." The transitional-being or "liminal persona" is defined by a name and by a set of symbols. The same name is very frequently employed to designate those who are being initiated into very different states of life. For example, amongst the Ndembu of Zambia the name *mwadi* may mean various things: it may stand for "a boy novice in circumcision rites," or "a chief-designate undergoing his installation rites," or, yet again, "the first or ritual wife" who has important ritual duties in the domestic family. Our own terms "initiate" and "neophyte" have a

similar breadth of reference. It would seem from this that emphasis tends to be laid on the transition itself, rather than on the particular states between which it is taking place (pp. 95–96).

CRISIS AS INITIATION

What a difference it would make if a person in the throes of a life crisis were called, as in the Ndembu tongue, a *mwadi*—an initiate— and then skillfully led to a rebirth. Instead, our psychological initiates are often labeled neurotic, psychotic, addictive or character-disordered, labels that create helplessness and low self-esteem. These labels reinforce the fearful story that we are damaged and less than whole, a belief that prevents accessing the First Stories of initiation that the universe provides to help us move out of liminality into rebirth.

Some of the power of twelve-step recovery programs comes from the context in which addiction is placed—the new stories that Bill W. created that echoed the truth of the First Stories. In anonymous programs, addictions are transitions between a life where the person was out of touch with a Higher Power and one in which the reality of that Power becomes not only the force for recovery but also a renewal of the meaning of life. Addiction as a *mwadi* experience, for those who are willing to see it in that light, creates a context of excitement, empowerment and even gratitude for the addiction as a conduit to a new, more self-aware and fulfilling life.

Psychological problems and addiction are not the only challenging life-events where context effects outcome. Psychiatrist Victor Frankl, in his moving book *Man's Search for Meaning*, talks about life in the Nazi death camps during the Holocaust. In those most terrible of times some people succumbed to the inevitable epidemics that swept the camp, dying before the brutality of the Nazis and the fire of the ovens could consume them. Others, those who were able to find some meaning in their suffering, were more likely to hold onto life. Frankl himself survived four death camps before liberation, and it was in those camps that he conceived of logotherapy, a system of psychological growth and healing based on the apprehension of meaning.

Frankl and others like him *created* ritual out of horror, growth out of destruction, by choosing to believe that there was some transcendent meaning to their suffering. When we set our sights on a higher meaning, we automatically cast ourselves in the role of a dweller at the threshold, an initiate in a Great Story. We are not powerless, trapped or worthless. We are passing through the fire on the way to a purification of sufficient value that our suffering becomes worthwhile when weighed against it. Part of the value of suffering and dwelling at the threshold is that it initiates or intensifies the search for what is most sacred, for only in placing our minds on the promise of that sacredness can we emerge from the liminal period not only intact but healed.

The late American psychologist Abraham Maslow spoke of the deep need to find in our lives not only personal meaning, but transpersonal or spiritual meaning. A need is like a biological drive, an instinct. It's part of the genes, part of the racial memories that form the collective unconscious that all people share. When a biological drive is thwarted the organism suffers in some way. The particular kind of suffering that accompanies a thwarted drive for transpersonal meaning is a feeling of emptiness, of meaningless about life that can progress to depression if the need is not attended to.

"Jack" was a patient of mine who came to therapy for just this reason. A tall, athletic man in his late forties, he was almost apologetic for taking up my time. "I'm not even sure why I'm here," he began. "I'm physically healthy, business is good, I've been married to a great lady for twenty-six years, and all the kids are out of the house and making a living." Jack paused to chuckle and reach for his wallet, producing one of those hospital photos of newborns that invariably resemble tadpoles caught in mid-metamorphosis. "How about this? I'm even a grandfather." Jack smiled as I bent over to admire the picture of his tiny new granddaughter.

As Jack replaced the picture and put his wallet away, his smile faded. "I should be happy, huh?" He paused as he searched for words, shaking his head and focusing his eyes inward. "Something is wrong. Something has changed, Joan, and I don't think it's age. I'm not having a mid-life crisis, worrying about my gray hairs or chasing younger women. I'm content with my life. I've got everything a guy could hope for. It's that, well . . . I used to like to get up in the morning. I looked forward to the day. Now, more and more, I wake up feeling, well," Jack searched for the right words again, "not exactly bored, but kind of empty. Kind of like, so what? Is this all there is? Is this all that life is about?"

I had reviewed the results of Jack's psychological testing before we met. Perfectly normal guy with a mild depression. Not a candidate for medication or even for psychotherapy, Jack was hungry for some kind of transpersonal meaning. His meaning drive was frustrated and he didn't know where to begin searching. We spent the next half hour talking about books, Boston-area personal growth centers, meditation practice, religion, spirituality and the growing men's movement.

I didn't see Jack again for about a year until we bumped into one another at a meditation workshop. He looked great. There was excitement in his eyes as he shared a little bit of the year's journey of self-discovery. He had taken up the regular practice of *vipassana*, or insight meditation, a form of awareness training from the Buddhist tradition that helps one to be present in the moment. Jack's growing ability to be "mindful," to be aware of his body, feelings, other people and nature had returned some of the richness to life that had been missing the year before. In addition, he had attended several meditation retreats with the poet, Buddhist teacher and peace worker Thich Nhat Hanh. The ideal of spiritual growth as compassionate action inherent in Buddhism had sparked Jack's interest in working actively in Amnesty International and volunteering time at a shelter for homeless men. The emptiness of which he had complained was filled to overflowing.

I believe that many cases of depression result from a thwarted need for meaning. Psychologists have defined many needs that motivate human behavior. The need for power, the need for achievement, the need for interpersonal closeness. When these needs are frustrated there is an increase in both psychological and physical symptoms. A frustrated need for transcendent meaning, in my experience, leads first to feelings of boredom and ennui such as Jack had. If these feelings are not attended to they are likely to get worse or to lead to second-order problems like addiction.

One of the ways people try to diminish discomfort is through alcohol and drugs. When an anxious or depressed person drinks, for example, therapists often refer to the behavior as "self-medicating." Although people escalate their drinking or drug-taking and develop addictions for a variety of different reasons, the dual qualities of pain relief and temporary reconnection to a state of enhanced perceptual awareness provide a type of ersatz or counterfeit spirituality that can suppress the underlying need for real spiritual reconnection. This is the reason why twelve-step programs, which are in part based on filling the need for authentic spirituality, are particularly helpful for people whose addiction stems from a frustrated need for spiritual meaning. These programs treat the cause, not just the symptoms, for this subset of people in recovery.

Frustrated needs for transpersonal meaning may lead not only to addiction but also to serious depression. In his book *A Confession*, Leo Tolstoy wrote of an incapacitating, existential depression that occurred in his late forties at a time when he was successful, healthy, enjoying a wonderful family life, wealth and considerable professional renown. In spite of it all Tolstoy felt lost and dejected, going through the motions of life like a sleepwalker and repeatedly asking himself questions very similar to Jack's. Is this all there is? What is life for?

When these existential questions begin to burn in our souls we can choose one of two roads. We can ignore them and become depressed, bored or addicted, or we can seize the challenge to explore our souls. It was in Tolstoy's seizing of the challenge that his writing became so penetrating, infused with the power of First Stories that he told in new, compelling ways.

A SPIRITUAL QUEST FOR MEANING— NEW STORIES

In *The Three Questions*, a short story, Tolstoy writes of a great king who is obsessed with finding answers to what he considers the three questions most important to being an effective ruler. Who is the most important person to be with? What is the most important thing to do? When is the most important time to do it?

As is typical of questing stories, all the great intellects and advisers of the land come up with conflicting answers, leaving the king to search for wisdom at a deeper well. The king then turns to a legendary wise person who lives a simple, hermit-like existence high on a mountaintop. Dressing as an ordinary traveler, the king leaves his soldiers a mile or two from the hermitage and continues the rest of the way up the mountain alone. He finds the old, bent wise man tilling his garden. The king announces the purpose of his visit and asks his three questions, but the old man just looks at him and asks for help with the gardening. The king wonders whether the wise man is for real or not, but holds his peace and helps the old man dig.

The strong young king soon tires and gets impatient for his answers, but as the old man continues to work through the heat of the day, so does the king. When the sun sets and the job is finally done the king is about to repeat his questions when a stranger stumbles out of the bushes, seriously wounded. The king rips off his shirt and staunches the flow of blood. He then carries the man into the hermit's house, cleans and bandages the wound and refreshes him with drink, saving his life.

The man is filled with both gratitude and shame, admitting to the king that he has followed him to the hermitage for the purpose of assassinating him on his way back down the mountain! But when the king was so long in coming, he left his hiding place, only to be discovered and wounded by the king's soldiers. The assassination attempt was an act of revenge on the king, who had killed the man's brother and taken the family lands. Upon hearing this account, the king is contrite. He admits his wrongdoing, restores and adds to the man's lands and pledges to be a better monarch. For his part, the man pledges to protect and support the king for all his life, and the two are reconciled.

The king emerges from this epiphany to find the hermit and get the answers to his questions. Who is the most important person to be with? What is the most important thing to do? When is the most important time to do it? The wise man smiles, assuring the king that he has already been given the answers. The king is perplexed, and the wise man is forced to voice what he considers the obvious. The most important person to be with is whoever you are with at any time. Had the king not been with the wise man tilling the garden all afternoon, he would have been killed by the assassin. The most important thing to do? To be of service to the one you're with, for in this way a blood feud was averted and forgiveness took place. And the most important time? Why now, of course, because in Tolstoy's words, "Now is the only time over which we have dominion."

In Tolstoy's story, the king was a dweller at the threshold who completed a rite of passage leading to wisdom. He left the robes and trappings of kingship down the mountain and sought answers humbled and stripped of presumptions. It was in the unaccustomed role of laborer and servant that he learned forgiveness and compassion. The king, like our friend Jack, was a fortunate man because he consciously sought for answers to questions of higher meaning. But even when we are not consciously seeking these answers, life keeps right on asking the questions, sometimes posing them with heart-stopping power by pulling the rug right out from under us.

DARK NIGHTS OF THE SOUL

Dark nights of the soul are extended periods of dwelling at the threshold when it seems as if we can no longer trust the very ground we stand on, when there is nothing familiar left to hold onto that can give us comfort. If we have a strong belief that our suffering is in the service of growth, dark night experiences can lead us to depths of psychological and spiritual healing and revelation that we literally could not have dreamed of and that are difficult to describe in words without sounding trite.

Had I not personally experienced two major dark nights and dozens of shorter threshold experiences, I wouldn't presume to write about them. To say that they are unpleasant is the same kind of understatement that labels labor pains "uncomfortable contractions." I've always thought that honesty is the best policy when describing pain. At forty, the time of my second dark night, I kept a journal. One entry read simply, "I'm terrified of my own terror. When I'm low it closes in on me and I can't get away. It's like facing your death—but *worse* since I know that even death is not an end. This must be hell. It feels like it could last for eternity. Is there any way out?"

At ten, during my first dark night experience, I kept no journal, but the memories are still vivid. The year was 1955. We had just moved across town, a distance of about five miles that might as well have been 5,000 miles to me because the familiar school, friends, apartment and neighborhood were gone. Gone, too, was Teresa the nanny (we called them nursemaids in the fifties), who, shy and distant though she was, had been the central pillar of a lonely childhood until she had married and gone off to start her own family just before we moved.

I was scared. Scared of the new school, scared I wouldn't make any new friends and scared of the strange stirrings in my body that were heralding the unfolding of womanhood. It felt like there was nothing familiar left to hold onto. Even the comfortable old bedspread of childhood had been consigned to the garbage. I arrived in my new room to find a decorator's vision of paradise suited to a New York career woman. Kelly-green custom bedspreads, matching drapes and sophisticated serographs topped off new mahogany furniture. No one had asked my opinion. I hated green. I hated the whole room, and I wasn't allowed to change anything or even to sit on the beds without removing the spreads because it would have spoiled the decor. The bedroom felt like a surrealistic Holiday Inn in which I was to reside as a permanent stranger, forever barred from leaving any sign of my occupancy.

Bizarre hallucinations and obsessions started almost immediately after the move. I would go to sleep in the strange room, in my strange body, in a strange life and be awakened by what I thought was the sound of tinkling glass. My ten-year-old mind had melded an episode of "Boston Blackie," a TV detective show of the fifties, and a movie about South American tribal life into a primitive landscape of horror. I imagined that headhunters with poison darts were cutting round circles out of windows all around the house and that they were going to kill my unsuspecting family.

I believed that only I could see what was happening and only I could save us from the terror of violent, frightening deaths. I was convinced that our salvation lay in my performance of strange, repetitive behaviors that mushroomed in number and complexity, as did my fantasies of destruction. In my mind scorpions, snakes and other poisonous creatures writhed in readiness, a breath away from jumping across a thin veil between the unmanifest realm and the actual living-room floor. It was up to me to prevent them from appearing in the flesh, dripping poison and death.

I developed the classic ritual behaviors that typify an obsessive-compulsive neurosis. I washed my hands dozens of times a day, partly out of a constant fear of being contaminated by poisons and partly as a ritual to keep the nightmare horrors from becoming real. My speech grew slow and tortured because I had to visualize every word I planned to speak and then

arrange
the
words
in
a
vertical
centered
mental
list
before
I
spoke.

Much of my reading had to be upside down and backward, and completed three times without interruption. If I was interrupted, I was sure that the nightmare creatures would come to life and kill us all. So I became wild-eyed with terror at any sign that I might not be able to complete the necessary ritual. I was sent home from school a few weeks into the illness when the math teacher took me to the nurse because I had become hysterical when she tried to collect a paper before I had completed the ritual of erasing each math problem three times before setting down the final answer. By the time we got to the nurse's office I imagined that my body was covered with tiny red marks from the poison darts of headhunters who were following me down the hall, dangerously close to coalescing out of the mists into solid physical form.

The nurse called my mother. It seemed as if they were both very angry with me for being a bad girl. The ultimate punishment was to be sent to a psychiatrist. I went feeling that I'd let my family down. I still remember sitting on a chair opposite his big desk. Filled with shame and a compensatory bravado, I informed him that I had come on a strictly social basis. He asked me a few questions and then settled me at a table, gave me crayons and left me alone to draw a picture. I drew a house with smoke curling tightly from the chimney. How I knew this I do not know, but I understood immediately that the tight curling of the smoke represented the rage I felt toward my mother for not allowing me to be myself. Not wanting to betray either her or myself (nice girls were not supposed to be angry, let alone enraged) I ripped the paper up.

The good doctor returned to see what I had produced. Rather self-righteously I informed him that I was on to his little tricks, that I knew he planned to analyze my drawings and that I considered him sneaky. If he wanted to know something about me, he should just ask. So we had a talk, and I actually liked him. I think I might eventually have been able to trust him. At the end of the hour, with my permission, he invited my mother in. He told her that I had too little freedom, I was too restricted. I should be allowed to express myself, to walk to the movies with friends, to choose my likes and dislikes. In her anguish and fear, mother became furious. "But I love her. I do everything for her own good. You psychiatrists are all alike, you always blame the mother."

As we left the psychiatrist's office, I knew that my mother wasn't going to take me back to him again. I believed that I would either die or get well. I also knew that I would have to go the distance unaided and alone. And so it is. In these experiences we either come out transformed or we die, literally or figuratively. During dark nights our belief system is challenged and we are thrust into mortal combat with the forces of our own and the collective unconscious. For a variety of different reasons—loss, guilt, trauma, shame, war, shock—

the world as we know it ceases to be and we are left with no familiar ground to stand on. A period of inner chaos characterized by fear, doubt, terror, depression or madness may follow.

The crisis resolves in one of three ways. After a period of suffering we slowly put ourselves back together again and life goes on in the same overtly or vaguely unsatisfactory way that it did before; we become so terrified, agitated or depressed that we commit suicide or stay in the desert of mental illness; or we come out transformed, emerging with a new strength, wisdom and vision. The questions we will be addressing in the remainder of the book have to do with how we can resolve the crises of liminal periods and dark nights in ways that lead to transformation.

My childhood dark night resolved itself in a most interesting way. Life had come to a standstill. As the weeks of torment and craziness turned to months, I finally had to leave school. After several days of absence, I had moved even further into a living hell that I no longer tried to explain to others. I was worn out, tired of the battle. How long can a solitary child hold off the legions of darkness?

Sometime during this period, I felt moved to write a poem. For me, poetry has always been the voice of my deepest feelings, my deepest truth. Even when our old self is dying, the immortal Self at our core is untouched by the pain. In fact, because our old perceptions no longer filter reality in the same way, communications from the wisdom Self sometimes come through more clearly in dreams, poems and insights. This particular poem popped into my mind one day as I sat on our porch, looking out over flower beds whose awakening presaged the coming summer.

The Light

Somewhere in the darkest night
There always shines
A small, bright light.
This light up in the heavens shines
To help our God watch over us.
When a small child is born

The light her soul does adorn.
But when our only human eyes
Look up in the lightless skies
We always know
Even though we can't quite see
That a little light
Burns far into the night
To help our God watch over us.

I recited this poem to myself often. It was all I had to hold onto other than periodic visits from my older brother, Alan, who was a student at Harvard at the time. He listened to me. He was there. I probably owe my life and sanity to a few conversations we had that he's probably long since forgotten. He was an island for me because our parents simply didn't know what to do. Since my mother's fear interfered with my getting professional help, I held myself together as best I could, no doubt adding to their denial of the seriousness of the situation.

Then, as the days of absence from school wore on, I realized that I might never recover. I might remain locked in hell for the rest of my life. It was already spring, and every summer I went to a Jewish girls' camp that I really loved. It was a place where I could be creative, where I was beginning to find out who I was. The knowledge that I might never go to the camp again, never sit in the pine grove and feel the peace and stillness, never chant the old prayers that had been an early spiritual experience for me, galvanized my will. I decided that either I would get better immediately, return to school, go to camp and pick up my life or I might as well die. I willed myself to hold my ground against the darkness, even if it resulted in death.

The next morning I got up and went to school. When the need to wash my hands became overwhelming, I just recited the poem. I was terrified, but terror was nothing new. It couldn't have been any worse than it already was. When I hallucinated the headhunters, I sat in my seat and did my work. If they got me, they got me. When I felt compelled to make a centered mental list of words before I spoke, I spoke anyway. I waited for the floor to bloom with serpents and spiders. It didn't. I waited for the headhunters to kill us all. They didn't. In a few days time the entire full-blown obsessive-compulsive neurosis had ended.

THE SELF

Obsessive-compulsive neurosis is a frequently intractable mental illness that can continue for a lifetime. On the other hand, for no known reason, it can sometimes go away on its own. It is often hereditary, and the rituals—like handwashing—so frequently resemble grooming behavior that some theorists believe that obsessive-compulsive disorder (OCD) is caused by a "tic" in the part of the brain that handles these instinctual behaviors. A drug called Anafranil, alone or with behavior therapy, can help about half of OCD patients. The remainder live difficult lives, often unable to function in school or job situations.

Psychiatrist Judith Rappoport increased public awareness of OCD exponentially with the publication of her fine book *The Boy Who Couldn't Stop Washing*. Like many people who had suffered this illness in isolation, I was fascinated to read the stories of other people like myself. As one man Dr. Rappoport interviewed put it, "One distressing aspect of my situation as a great ritualist was my certainty that I was the only person on earth who suffered, had ever suffered, would ever suffer as I did. I could not talk to anyone about my rituals or my fears. I was scared and mortified."

Whether one theorizes that my OCD was brought on by the trauma of a move, the lack of freedom to be myself or a tic in the brain—it was certainly a major rite of passage. I believe that my cure, which was immediate and dramatic, was guided by the part of me that wrote the poem and was in turn accessed by the poem—my Higher Self. Many modern psychologists, including C. G. Jung, Roberto Assagioli and Abraham Maslow, advocated a psychology of potential based on realizing the Self, on living from that creative core of being. This is a departure from psychologies where no Self is posited and in which "normality," Freud's ordinary state of unhappiness, is the highest we can aspire to.

Maslow pointed out that we connect with a higher Self during what he called "peak experiences," those moments when we feel completely absorbed in the present—transported by nature, delighted by a child, carried off in a creative high, transformed by love. During these moments of wholeness—or holy moments, as I like to think of them—we feel joy, peace, security, unity, harmony, love, sacredness and a vibrant sense of aliveness. These are the moments that make life worth living, moments that are direct answers to the questions "Why am I here?" and "What is the meaning of life?"

While everyone connects with their higher nature once in a while, Maslow found that some people spend considerable time in this state. Rather than being hostage to the lower nature with its doubts and fears, such "self-actualizers" are more loving, forgiving, delightful and balanced than the norm. In his landmark book *A Psychology of Being*, Maslow says of self-actualization:

> We may define it as an episode, or a spurt in which the powers of the person come together in a particularly efficient and intensely enjoyable way, and in which he is more integrated and less split, more open for experience, more idiosyncratic, more perfectly expressive or spontaneous, or fully functioning, more creative, more humorous, more ego-transcending, more independent of his lower needs, etc. He becomes in these episodes more truly himself, more perfectly actualizing his potentialities, closer to the core of his Being, more fully human (p. 96).

Maslow's definition of being centered in the Self as feeling more integrated and less split was precisely my experience as a ten-year-old when I created the "Light" poem and later, when I recited it to myself to take courage in overcoming my compulsive behaviors. The dark night experience, in contrast, was one of complete fragmentation where the center that held my personality together was lost.

The most graphic example of fragmentation is the clinical syndrome of multiple personality disorder (MPD), in which the patient has no stable sense of self. Instead, the personality consists of multiple, separate selves, each formed at a particular time during childhood, generally as a result of severe physical or sexual abuse or the witnessing of terrible trauma, such as violent death or torture.

An imaginative child will often dissociate—space out—during a terrifying or painful situation. These dissociative episodes can become more real than what is happening, literally taking on a life of their own. As a result, the child may develop several different personalities, or "alters." Research indicates that the average number of alters in a person with MPD is thirteen. One may emerge to take physical abuse, another to care for siblings, a third to go to school, a fourth to be available for incestual sex, a fifth to be "the protector" and so on. These alters are not only psychologically distinct in terms of having their own life history, they are also physiologically different. One may be allergic or need glasses while the others do not. One may be right-handed while the others are left-handed. There are even anecdotal reports that when one alter is a substance abuser, only that personality will undergo withdrawal.

Under hypnosis it is often possible for the alters to remember the exact moment of their "birth." In the early 1970s therapist Dr. Ralph Allison reported the existence of a special personality that was potentially present in each person with multiple personality disorder. Unlike the others, it had no interest in taking over the body and ruling the roost. Its only interest was in the integration of all the fragmented personalities into a healthy, functional whole. In fact, it was often an important source of help with the therapy and for that reason Allison called it the Inner Self-Helper.

When asked about its origin, the Inner Self-Helper told a consistent story in each individual where it could be accessed. It said, in essence, "I have always been," describing itself as an immortal presence that existed before physical birth and would continue to exist after bodily death. The Inner Self-Helper is devoid of fear, guilt, hatred, anger, doubt or depression. Kind, wise, loving and compassionate, this core personality sometimes describes itself as a conduit for God's love. Dr. Willis Harman, president of the Institute for Noetic Sciences, notes that descriptions of the Inner Self-Helper parallel ancient descriptions of the Self from Eastern texts. The Upanishads are one of the cornerstones of India's wisdom tradition, dating back to between 1500 and 5000 B.C. The Katha Upanishad states:

The Self . . . is not born. It does not die. It is neither cause nor effect. This Ancient One is unborn, imperishable; though the body be destroyed, it is not killed . . . Smaller than the smallest, greater than the greatest, this Self forever dwells within the hearts of all.

Ancient philosophy is very similar to newly emergent transpersonal psychologies in describing psychological health as the ability to live from the true Self rather than from false selves that form to protect us from fear. In the extreme case of multiple personality disorder, fear gives rise to totally separate personalities, yet this is just an extreme version of what we consider normal. We all have different ego states, different subpersonalities. The perfectionist, the self-critic, the victim, the rescuer, the hero, the complainer, the self-destroyer— these are common false selves that arise in reaction to childhood fears, as I discuss in depth in *Guilt Is the Teacher, Love Is the Lesson*. These different selves are clearly not who we really are; they are just the familiar masks we wear in certain situations because they made us feel safe as children.

By the time I was a ten-year-old fighting the demons of darkness, my mask was pretty well formed. Little Miss Goody-goody was polite, shy and perfectionistic. My room was neat, my homework was done in advance and I took lots of lessons after school. But the most interesting parts of me had been tucked away in that backwater of consciousness that Jung called the shadow and that the poet Robert Bly calls the "long bag we drag behind us." In the bag are all the things that someone whose approval we needed as children told us were not good enough. So the bag is full of emotions, talents and thoughts that are expressions of our uniqueness. It's full of the wild and juicy stuff.

My own shadow was full of songs that my voice wasn't "good enough" to sing and pictures that my talent was too spare to paint. It was full of long hair, dangly earrings and leather sandals that were decidedly "unladylike." It was also full of rage for being shamed and grief that I could not be appreciated for who I was. The rage fueled rebellious fantasies about escape and revenge. In my imagination I would run away to New York City where I would support myself in a dance hall and marry a sailor. That would show my mother a thing or two!

Needless to say, if we act out of the shadow our acts are often self-destructive. That's one very good reason to explore the shadow, the inner darkness that teams with emotions, fantasies and talents. To the degree that we are out of touch with the shadow energies we are incomplete. We are living from a false self while the creative energies languish. Furthermore, if we don't empty the shadow bag, the contents will compost and build up steam. We can relieve the pressure by projecting the contents of the shadow on others, seeing other people as angry or jealous because we can't stand to see these emotions in ourself. But if we do this then we end up going through life literally being scared of our own shadow. We can also relieve the pressure by splitting off the contents of the shadow in a more dramatic way—into headhunters, snakes and scorpions or, as the good Dr. Jekyll did, on to our own personal Mr. Hyde!

As Jung remarked, "One does not become enlightened by imagining figures of light, but by making the darkness conscious." At no time are we more conscious of the darkness than in the midst of a dark night of the soul. And at no other time are we less conscious of the light, although it has never abandoned us. In its concealment it forces us to stand on the threshold and commit ourselves to becoming new. If we can trust and believe that our dark night has come in service of the light, then we can breathe through the transition and do the work that is necessary to prepare for the birth.

CHAPTER FOUR

What If?—
Reframing Basic Beliefs

Truly, it is in the darkness that one finds the light, so when we are in sorrow, then this light is nearest of all to us.

Meister Eckhart

Just prior to Christmas 1985 I discovered a lump in my breast. It was suspicious enough to require surgical removal. During the week before the surgery my thoughts kept coming back to the question "What if" over and over again. "What if the lump turns out to be nothing?" was a question I asked only once because it didn't lead to ruminating. What my mind got stuck on were the ramifications of the question "What if the lump turns out to be cancer?" This answer gave rise to a whole host of other "What ifs?" What if it has spread, what if I need chemotherapy, what if I die?

The "What ifs?" in turn led me to consider the meaning of the hypothetical cancer. Was it, indeed, an awakening experience, an archetypal dark night of the soul that would enrich my life, inform my faith and lead to freedom, what I called a First Story in the parable? Or was this fantasized disaster a meaningless event in a random universe? Worse still, was it all my fault—the result of negative thinking, punishment for my sins or the return of "bad karma"? Thankfully, the lump turned out to be benign. And, although

I suffered considerably as a result of the stories I entertained about its meaning, I learned a lot about my most basic beliefs.

Now that we have had the opportunity to consider how we formulate our belief systems and develop faith, I invite you to consider some nonfearful alternatives to the question of why bad things happen by reframing fearful "What ifs?" into more hopeful, realistic alternatives. After each invitation to consider a new "What if," there is an affirmation. If it feels good, try repeating it out loud.

What if you were a fragment of a larger consciousness? Such a fragment can be thought of as a creative impulse that is at once unique yet made of the same essence as all other souls. As a one-time medical scientist, I like this metaphor. All the cells of our body—eyes, ears, heart, muscles, liver and so on—are encoded with the full intelligence of the body. Hypothetically an entire replica, or clone, of the body could be grown from a single cell. Similarly, the creative intelligence of the Universe is perfectly present in each of its parts. We are like holograms of the One Mind.

I am a child of the One Light
The wisdom of the Universe is present within me.

What if the One Mind knows itself through its creations? The same lifeforce that grows an oak from an acorn, a mountain from the earth's molten core, a stream from the spring thaw, a child from an egg and a sperm, an idea from the mind of a human being is present in all things, all thoughts and all experiences. There is no place where God is not. The One Mind lives its Stories and knows itself through perceiving the reflections it creates, yet it is simultaneously present in those reflections.

God is present in all things, all experiences.
The Universe knows itself and expands itself through me.

What if the purpose of my existence is to become truly loving, and through that love find my way back to the divine source. Think about those times in which you have felt most fully human—present to a sunset, aware of the light in the eyes of a child, being kind or helpful with no thought of return, filled with the peace that comes from forgiveness. In these loving moments we feel connected to a greater whole. Love is the topic of many of the First Stories that were left to guide us home: the forgiving love of the father for the Prodigal Son, the blissful love of the gopis for the Lord Krishna, the pure and devoted love of Mary Magdalene for Jesus. The simple love of the prince who awakens Snow White from a deathlike sleep.

I am ready to wake up now.
My Higher Self is full of love stories.

What if we find our freedom through struggling against darkness. Where would Luke Skywalker be without Darth Vader? How would Jacob have walked across the Jabbok River to claim his new life without first wrestling with the angel who crippled his thigh? Would Camelot have been so sweet if Arthur had been handed it on a silver platter? Dark nights can awaken First Stories of freedom, or they can reinforce the belief that we are powerless. The choice for bondage or freedom is ours. This is called free will.

Darkness is the great awakener.
In facing adversity I can find my freedom.

What if you were immortal. Imagine that the suit of flesh you are currently sitting in is a spacesuit that you need in order to venture into an alien world. You have temporarily forgotten that you put this suit on to have an adventure and actually believe that the suit is who you are! Imagine your surprise at the moment of "death." Your suit falls off, its purpose complete, and your soul rises back into the presence of the Light from which you emerged. There, in the presence of overwhelming love, you are helped to review this life—which seems much like a dream when it's over—and evaluate the stories you have spun. Were they stories of love and freedom, or did you fall asleep and dream stories of fear?

I can wake up now.
I can choose to believe in love over fear.

What if those things that seem unfair turn out to make sense? According to those who have returned from near-death experiences, it is there in the presence of the Light that we understand the circumstances of our life. Everything makes sense and we seem to have had exactly the adventure that our soul required to find its way back to the Source. If we had previously—in other lives and other realms of being—created stories of fear that hid the First Stories of love, we had to face those fears and overcome them.

I am given the circumstances I require for my awakening.
Every situation, seen rightly, contains the seeds of freedom.

What if you have all the help you need to find your way back to the Light? Your own Higher Self and your guides—teachers and comforting presences in the nonphysical realm who accompany you throughout life (some people think of these beings as guardian angels)—are always trying to get your attention. Many people who have had near-death experiences meet these guides when they are out of their bodies and subsequently maintain a conscious communication with them. But whether you are conscious of them or not, they are always trying to communicate with you.

All the help I need is available to me.
I can receive it by asking.

What if pain is also an act of service. When your own heart has been broken you are most empathetic to the suffering of others. You then become what Thornton Wilder called a "soldier in love's service." Only those "broken by the wheels of living," said Wilder, could serve in this way. A mother who has lost her son can become a special beacon of hope to other bereaved parents. A person who is living well with cancer, or who has recovered against all odds, is uniquely helpful to others traveling the same territory. One who has suffered incest or been betrayed, brutalized or abandoned and has set herself or

himself free through forgiveness is especially able to help others learn
how to forgive.

> *The power to love and serve grows through pain.*
> *I can offer healing to others as I heal myself.*

PART TWO

The Transformation of Fear

I sat silent by the Great River
and wondered at the
reflections
of the willow branches
dancing in its darkness.

Small mind closed like a fist
around the image of
snakes
writhing a mysterious
death dance in the deep.

Big mind opened like blue sky
and welcomed the
play
of Love's creation stories
unfolding in the mirror.

J. Z. B.

CHAPTER FIVE

Fear, Trauma and Transformation

Fear Not.
What is not real, never was and never will be.
What is real, always was and cannot be destroyed.

Bhagavad Gita

One May in the early 1980s I was visiting New York City, speaking at a conference on psychoneuroimmunology at the New York Academy of Medicine. An old friend was also at the conference, and at the end of the day we wandered outside into the late afternoon sunshine. Finding an empty bench just outside of Central Park, we put our luggage down and were soon engaged in rapt conversation. Perhaps an hour passed. Unfortunately, in our intense mindfulness of each other, we were totally unmindful of the changes taking place on the street around us. The daytime working crowd had dispersed and a more predatory nighttime population was emerging. We must have looked like sitting ducks with our high heels and heavy suitcases.

We were jarred from our reverie when two tall youths approached and asked for the time. Then, with either a finger or a gun in a pants pocket, one of them demanded that we hand over our jewelry and our purses. I am a great believer in intuition, and mine instantly yelled, "Don't worry, it's a finger!" So I jumped up screaming and chased the would-be muggers into Central Park (still hanging onto my suitcase for fear someone else would snatch it), hoping that someone speedier or better armed than I would apprehend the two young ruffians.

My colleague responded to the would-be robbery with equal courage. She scanned the situation and, for whatever reason (most of my friends mention sanity), chose freeze-or-submit rather than fight-or-flight. Had my intuition not been so strong and insistent, my nervous system might have made the same choice hers did. In these kinds of situations decisions come from the gut, not the intellect. When we are faced with a physical threat, it is fear that mobilizes us to survive and informs our courage. One good scare and the heart races, the breath becomes fast and shallow, and we develop almost superhuman strength as an outpouring of adrenaline shifts metabolism into high gear and pours sugar and oxygen into the furnace of our muscles. Fear mobilizes our resources to survive. It was this "emergency response" that allowed me to give chase to our would-be muggers while toting a heavy suitcase.

Like other pack animals, human beings are wired to attack when the odds of winning are good and to freeze when they are not. Freezing is a sign of submission and sometimes calls off attack. I have no doubt that the courage needed to preserve one's physical life under sudden attack is far less complicated than the courage to make the moral and ethical choices that elevate civilization above animal instinct. But before we consider these higher order forms of courage in the next chapter, let's take a closer look at what our ordinary and extraordinary fears are made of.

WHAT DO WE FEAR?

The most basic fear of every human being is rooted in the helplessness of childhood, the time before we are capable of surviving on our own and must depend on the protection of powerful others. It is the fear of rejection and abandonment. This instinctual terror arises from the part of the mind that thinks not in words but in feelings and images. The common nightmares that children have about being chased and devoured by monsters—nightmares that occur even in children who have never been exposed to the idea of a monster—are the expression of a primitive fear that has its roots at the dawn of human history when abandoned children were, indeed, chased and devoured by wild animals.

The consequences of emotional abandonment are no less serious than those of physical abandonment. Babies in foundling homes that are fed and changed on schedule but starved emotionally often develop a syndrome called hospitalism or failure to thrive. No one is present to coo when baby coos, to smile when baby smiles, to mirror back its existence to the child. As a result of this loneliness, the babies' pituitary glands fail to produce sufficient growth hormone and the children wither away despite adequate nutrition. Many of these children die before reaching toddlerhood, and those who do survive are often severely damaged psychologically. They cannot bond with other human beings.

Lonely adults are also at risk physically. Heart disease and immunological deficits are associated with loneliness. Widowed, single and divorced men suffer more illness and death than married men, and large, epidemiological studies indicate that the single best predictor of good health for both sexes is social support, a caring network of family and/or friends. To be isolated is the greatest tragedy for a human being and the most generic form of stress. The interested reader can find an excellent review of the effects of isolation on general health and on the cardiovascular system in *Dr. Dean Ornish's Program for Reversing Coronary Artery Disease*. I agree with Dr. Ornish that the three levels at which human beings experience isolation and the fear and stress that accompany it are:

The personal level. The universal psychological wound of Western culture is unworthiness, the soul sickness of low self-esteem that underlies psychological and religious pessimism. Most people are fiercely self-critical, having internalized the shaming voices of their parents. They secretly believe that whatever they do is not good enough, that other people would not like them if they really knew them, that they are selfish, bad or simply not as competent as others.

The interpersonal level. To the extent that we can't accept ourselves we will also have trouble acknowledging and encouraging the potential in other people. Instead, our relationships will tend to be an unconscious replay of the old wounds to our self-worth projected onto others, and true intimacy will remain an impossibility.

The transpersonal level. When we cannot celebrate ourselves, neither can we come into union with the Absolute, believing that we are unworthy to enter the bridal chamber of which the mystics of all traditions, including Jesus, speak.

And if we cannot feel the love of God because we cannot love ourselves, how can we be happy? How can we be grateful? The spiritual core of religions as seemingly diverse as those of various Native American nations, Hinduism, Buddhism, Judaism and Christianity is thanksgiving. According to the Greek Orthodox tradition, for example, the role of humankind is to reflect the glory of creation back to the Creator. The Greek Orthodox priest Saint John of Kronstadt said, "If I do not feel a sense of joy in God's creation, if I forget to offer the world back to God with thankfulness, I have advanced very little upon the Way. I have not yet learned to be truly human. For it is only through thanksgiving that I can become myself."

Most people can remember moments when they suddenly transcended their isolation and felt connected to a center of love and strength deep within. These peak experiences or holy moments are characterized by a profound sense of unity with nature, other people or the Universe: being fully present to a sunset, seeing an old person and feeling tears of love well up in our eyes, seeing the light reflected from a spider's web, holding our child at the moment of his birth, holding our mother at the moment of her death, forgiving someone and, in that instant, feeling at one with them. These experiences of connectedness are freely given states of grace.

At such moments we are in touch with our own true natures, and there is absolutely and positively no fear. Fear cannot exist where there is connectedness because the core of fear is isolation. While these moments of grace overcome most of us from time to time, raining down some relief on our parched souls, it is in facing the fears that normally keep us isolated that we heal. In so doing, we find gratitude, happiness and freedom.

FACING PERSONAL FEARS

Some fears are person-specific and learned. They are related to particular traumatic or frightening circumstances that permanently imprint danger signals onto our nervous systems. For example, my father feared dogs for most of his life because he had an early memory of watching a dog bite his mother. My early memories of dogs were delightful, so I grew up loving them. Fear of dogs is not an instinctual memory; it is an idiosyncratic experience. My father's fear of dogs was so strong that it kept him from buying a house for many years since he was afraid that the neighbors might own a dog. Similarly, a college friend of mine had a morbid fear of rodents and had to abandon a major in psychology because the classrooms and the rat rooms were in too close proximity.

Acquired fears, such as phobias of dogs, rats, snakes, bridges, water and the like, can often be effectively treated with a simple psychological procedure called systematic desensitization in which the person practices consciously relaxing while imagining progressively more frightening aspects of the phobia. A person who is afraid of dogs, for example, might first practice relaxing while imagining that he is looking at a picture of a dog. When this step is mastered, he might imagine seeing a puppy behind the window of a pet store. The next step might be to imagine patting the dog while someone else is holding it. When the person can remain relaxed while imagining that he is patting the dog, he can practice the desensitization in real life, gradually working up to patting a real puppy.

A variety of behavioral techniques—including relaxation, belly breathing, reframing the meaning of the fear and paying close attention to, rather than avoiding, fear—are discussed in detail in my first book, *Minding the Body, Mending the Mind*. These techniques are frequently helpful not only for isolated phobias, but also for generalized, immobilizing fears like agoraphobia in which a person may be literally terrified to leave the house.

Deeper fears, arising from severe emotional or physical abuse, incest, war or other trauma usually require more sophisticated behavioral and psychological treatment. The phenomenon of post-traumatic stress disorder that occurred in many Vietnam veterans has alerted therapists to the occurrence of this disorder in people whose battleground was the family living room or bedroom. Therapists are just beginning to develop treatments for their terrible traumas, as we will consider later in the chapter, after we have had a chance to consider creative strategies for dealing with less disabling types of fear.

It is prudent to attend to all levels of fear—physical, psychological and spiritual. Whether or not the fear has an archetypal, initiative quality or purpose, it may also convey important information about environment or life-style. People sometimes make mistakes in seeking or not seeking treatment for their fears because they pigeonhole them as "spiritual" and necessary medication as "material." Conversely, they may use medication to cover up fear that can be a clue about the necessity for a psychospiritual healing. But before looking for the deeper roots of fear, it is important to consider the role of heredity (some depressions and anxiety disorders are inherited biochemical blueprints that need biochemical treatment), life-style and addiction as common contributors to fear.

The Question of Medication

Some people make the mistake of thinking that medication is a sign of failure or an antispiritual strategy. This is emphatically not the case. While in general medication is certainly overprescribed, its judicious use is sometimes required either for brief periods while a person mobilizes the resources to cope, or for longer periods if true biochemical disturbances exist. Certain forms of serious depression, for example, may be accompanied by extreme anxiety. While I have had a few patients in this state who were able to use diaphragmatic breathing and meditation to calm themselves, more frequently psychiatric help and medication were necessary to take the edge off the fear before the person was calm enough to even use these techniques.

After breathing and meditation became familiar, it was then often possible to gradually diminish medication under supervision.

Medication may be required for extended periods in some instances of depression, manic depression or psychosis, which are often related to inherited biochemical disbalances that require medication not to cover up symptoms but to restore nervous system functioning to normal.

When people who need the help are reluctant to take medication I often remind them of the joke about the farmer and the flood. When the waters got to the farmer's bottom windows, a neighbor rowed over to rescue him. The farmer declined, "I'm a man of faith. God will rescue me." When the water rose to the second-story windows, another neighbor appeared in a motorboat. Again the farmer declined to be rescued, "I'm a man of faith. God will save me." Finally, as the farmer sat on his roof, a helicopter flew over and lowered a ladder. Once again the farmer declined, "I'm a man of faith. I'm certain that God will save me." The next thing he knew, the farmer found himself at the pearly gates. "What happened," he moaned to Saint Peter. "Why didn't God save me?" Saint Peter shook his head sadly, saying, "Listen here, we sent a rowboat, a motorboat and a helicopter!"

What is it about medication that some people think is unsacred?

Looking to First Things First

Sometimes fear has little or nothing to do with a biochemical disorder requiring medication or with psychological or spiritual matters. Instead, it can be a symptom of simple physiological imbalance. "Sally," a young woman in her twenties, came to me to learn diaphragmatic breathing and other physiological self-regulation strategies in the hope that it would alleviate her chronic anxiety. But when I took a history of her life-style and health behaviors, we decided together that she would make a few basic changes before beginning such a program. Sally's morning routine consisted of rolling out of bed with just enough time to shower, dress and stop at the local doughnut shop for a large coffee and two doughnuts before work. She continued to drink highly sweetened coffee throughout the day, about eight cups on the average. The only exercise she got was teetering from her office to the parking garage in high-heeled shoes.

Sally committed to weaning herself gradually from the caffeine, decreasing a cup per day each week to avoid caffeine-withdrawal headaches. She also agreed to get up forty-five minutes earlier, which allowed her time to take a thirty-minute walk and then eat a nutritious high-carbohydrate, low-fat breakfast of oatmeal, whole-grain bread, unsweetened jam and fruit. She also bought lower-heeled shoes that decreased the strain on her spine and supported a more relaxed pattern of breathing. Two months later, Sally's anxiety was practically gone. In her case the most creative response to overcoming fear was a change in life-style.

Paying Attention to Addiction

Even though the recovery movement has burgeoned in the last decade, addiction is a frequently overlooked source of anxiety and/or depression, both for the addict and for his or her loved ones. One in ten Americans are alcoholics, and significantly more people are directly affected by the alcoholism of a close friend or loved one. Psychotherapy has a poor track record in the treatment of addictions, as C. G. Jung himself found out when he treated Bill W., one of the cofounders of the Alcoholics Anonymous self-help fellowship. Jung wrote a now-famous letter to Bill W., stating that alcoholism was too deeply seated to be cured by psychological means and that Bill W.'s hopes lay in a spiritual conversion. He had that conversion, of course, and out of it came the twelve-step programs that have been called the greatest spiritual force in America today.

The power of twelve-step programs is multifaceted. Hearing the stories of other recovering alcoholics is inspiring, and a body of simple wisdom and profound truths have emerged from those in recovery. The slogans "One day at a time," "Live and let live" and "Let go and let God" are solid principles for anyone seeking to live a happy, well-balanced life. Admitting one's powerlessness over the addiction, asking a Higher Power for help, practicing the steps of taking responsibility for one's actions and learning to forgive are also integral parts of the program. The commitment of people in twelve-step recovery programs to helping others gain and maintain sobriety has led to a network of people involved in authentic personal and spiritual growth that crosses the lines of class and color. Help is also available for friends and family of alcoholics through Al-Anon.

Because alcohol is an anesthetic, people who are fearful or depressed are at high risk for becoming alcohol dependent because they use it as a form of medication to dull their uncomfortable feelings. When the addiction finally makes life unmanageable, because it results in behavior that is hurtful to self and others, the addict frequently has the experience of hitting bottom. A car crash, troubles at work, getting fired, going to jail, children who follow suit and become alcoholic or drug dependent, a wife or a husband who uses tough love and says, "This is it. I'm leaving. I can't live with your alcoholism anymore"—these are common experiences of bottoming out and true dark nights of the soul that are a challenge to rebirth.

THE NIGHTMARE OF ABUSE AND TRAUMA

In addition to the common sources we have just considered, there is another common source of fear that has been largely overlooked and minimized until the last decade—severe trauma. Child and adult experiences of sexual abuse, physical abuse and other exposures to violence can create profound isolation. In the case of sociopaths who were so seriously abused in their childhood that they can maim and kill other people with no compunction, the ability to connect with others is essentially lost. To some degree all victims of trauma suffer from the soul sickness of isolation, which, as we will see, can require heroic and creative treatment to heal.

When Sigmund Freud first reported that a significant number of his patients claimed to have been molested by fathers, brothers, uncles and family friends, his colleagues did not believe him. How could these sordid reports be true of the straitlaced, Victorian upper crust? His own belief in the reports of his patients shaken by the cold reception of his colleagues, Freud sketched a more palatable explanation for these incestuous stories—fantasy and wish fulfillment. Unfortunately for his patients and their painful secrets, Freud was mistaken in not continuing to take their claims seriously. It is currently estimated that 20 to 25 percent of women and 10 to 15 percent of men were sexually molested as children. The majority of women in prisons and more than 90 percent of those in mental institutions are believed to be victims of childhood sexual abuse.

Some of these women and men consciously remember the abuse and others do not. It is common for highly charged traumatic material to be pushed back so far into the unconscious that it is no longer available to memory. When a cue that might remind the person of the trauma is perceived (for example, a man walking down the street is the spitting image of the next-door neighbor who was the molester), the memory of the trauma may remain repressed while intense fear is felt. For no apparent reason, the person is overtaken by panic, dread or the urge to run. Suddenly he or she is hyperventilating. The usual treatment for these unprovoked panic attacks is to try and medicate them away, or to breathe into a paper bag to inhibit the hyperventilation.

Several patients to whom I have taught breathing techniques to calm hyperventilation have suddenly retrieved memories of abuse. Such memories are called *state dependent*. That is, retrieving them is conditional on being in the same physiological state as when the memory was imprinted onto the nervous system. In the office, when asked to hyperventilate, the patient may suddenly recall a trauma. In my experience, many women with so called fibrositis, a nonspecific chronic pain syndrome, are survivors of childhood sexual or physical abuse, as are a significant number of people, men and women alike, who suffer from panic attacks of unexplained origin.

In cases where current fear is related to childhood abuse, the most creative strategy for dealing with the fear is healing the old memories of abuse rather than continuing to cover them up. This entails facing the original pain, recognizing that a child is powerless and is not responsible for having been abused, owning the rage and terror that was caused by the abuse, confronting parents and/or abusers when appropriate, reparenting the frightened inner child (as I discuss in *Guilt is the Teacher, Love is the Lesson*) and finally reaching a state of forgiveness based on a personal transformation. As we will discuss in later chapters, forgiveness in no way means condoning the abuser.

Acts of abuse were and always will be an abomination. Forgiveness means coming to some understanding of why abusive people abuse— it is usually out of their own pain and abuse—and coming to some closure that sets one free from the hatred that gives the abuser continuing power.

When childhood abuse is severe and the child is particularly imaginative, multiple personality disorder (MPD) may develop. When panic attacks or psychosomatic illnesses are accompanied by symptoms such as blackouts (unaccounted for by alcoholism or drug addiction), sudden and dramatic switches in personality or substantial periods of lost time during which there is no memory of what has happened, the explanation may be MPD. As recently as five years ago many therapists knew little about MPD, childhood incest and molestation, childhood physical abuse, adult children of dysfunctional backgrounds and the relation of these syndromes to fear and panic states. The effects of trauma were also often overlooked in adults.

Adult survivors of holocausts, torture, war, natural disasters, violent crimes, serious accidents, fires, or any other traumatic incidents that are outside the range of usual human experience may develop post-traumatic stress disorder (PTSD). Symptoms may include a kind of psychic numbing or tuning out to the world so that previous sources of pleasure no longer seem interesting, emotions are dulled and it is difficult to feel close to another person. Depression, fear, hyperventilation, a racing heart, sweaty palms, jumpiness and other indications of increased sympathetic nervous system arousal are common, as are flashbacks to the trauma, repetitive nightmares about the event and guilt for surviving a situation where others died or were more seriously injured. Oddly, although PTSD usually begins at the time of the trauma, it is not uncommon for it to emerge several years later.

The stark reality that more Vietnam veterans died from suicide after the war than were killed during the war points to the seriousness of PTSD. Add to the suicides the fact that a significant proportion of our country's homeless are traumatized Vietnam veterans and the scope of this problem begins to emerge. Therapists are still searching for techniques to alleviate PTSD, which is often chronically disabling and difficult to treat. Clues to new kinds of treatment that may prove helpful come from two unusual sources: the shamans or native healers of indigenous cultures, and LSD-assisted psychotherapy, which is unfortunately banned almost entirely in the United States but, as we'll see in following sections, is being pursued abroad.

THE JOURNEY THROUGH THE BELLY OF THE BEAST

In order to structure a framework for the transformational healing of trauma, we must once again look deep into the human unconscious, to those archetypal Stories that transcend barriers of time and culture. In *The Power of Myth,* Joseph Campbell speaks to the universal significance of Jonah's terrifying experience when he was swallowed up into the belly of an enormous whale:

> The belly is the dark place where digestion takes place and new energy is created. The story of Jonah in the whale is an example of a mythic theme that is practically universal, of the hero going into a fish's belly and ultimately coming out again, transformed. . . .
>
> Psychologically, the whale represents the power of life locked in the unconscious. Metaphorically, water is the unconscious, and the creature in the water is the life or energy of the unconscious, which has overwhelmed the conscious personality and must be disempowered, over-come and controlled.
>
> In the first stage of this kind of adventure, the hero leaves the realm of the familiar, over which he has some measure of control, and comes to a threshold, let us say the edge of a lake or sea, where a monster of the abyss comes to meet him. . . . In a story of the Jonah type, the hero is swallowed and taken into the abyss later to be resurrected—a variant of the death-and-resurrection theme. The conscious per-sonality here has come in touch with a charge of uncon-scious energy which it is unable to handle and must now

suffer all the trials and revelations of a terrifying night-sea journey, while learning how to come to terms with this power of the dark and emerge, at last, to a new way of life (p. 146).

This archetypal experience of meeting the darkness, the powerful unconscious in which the lifeforce dwells, is indeed terrifying, as I found during my own descent into those dragon-infested waters as a ten-year-old suffering from obsessive-compulsive disorder. During those months I dreamed a repetitive nightmare that recapitulated the story of Jonah. In the dream I leaped into a lake, leaving the known world behind, and at the point of least safety—midway between two rafts in deep water—was confronted by an enormous serpent that arose from the deep to consume me. Waking in terror, I had no way of knowing that my experience had ever been shared by another human being. Had I known that at ten, and had I been guided by a therapist who knew that, I might have been able to claim the power of the unconscious much earlier.

When I later discovered that the nightmares and other aspects of my obsessive-compulsive disorder were written of in biblical stories and mythology, I was able to understand and integrate my illness as an experience in soul growth rather than as a meaningless bout with madness. A wound with meaning is much easier to heal than a wound that is meaningless or that, worse, is interpreted as divine punishment or other evidence of personal unworthiness.

Serious illnesses, traumas, archetypal nightmares of death and resurrection, and periods of madness are also described in accounts of shamanic initiation. A shaman is a healer who is able to access the realm of the collective unconscious, where the First Stories reside. As we will discuss in the following chapters, this realm of mind is also the level on which near-death experiences occur and where the soul is believed to reside when it is not embodied. Shamans from some cultures believe that when we suffer trauma part of our souls actually leave our bodies and must be retrieved from this realm if we are to recover our sanity, and often our health.

While the metaphoric journey of death and resurrection occurs in

First Stories from all cultures, that shared journey can also be tapped from the unconscious of people who serve as research subjects for the investigation of the psychoactive substance LSD. Psychiatrist Stanislav Grof was one of the researchers selected by the Swiss pharmaceutical company Sandoz to assess the effects of diethylamide lysergic acid (LSD-25) in the 1950s. He discovered that under the influence of the drug, people reexperienced the archetypal themes of trial and redemption, birth and death, union and separation, love and fear that occur in the myths and holy scriptures of all cultures.

By the time I had heard of LSD in the mid-1960s, Grof and other researchers had been investigating its effects for a decade, mapping out regions of the collective unconscious that supercede our personal histories and tell universal stories. These regions are not uniquely tapped by LSD. They have been described in accounts of psychotic states that stem from schizophrenia and temporal lobe epilepsy, in reports of naturally occurring visions and in the religious and mystical literature of both East and West. These experiences may include realistic encounters with angels and demons, wisdom guides and heavenly judges; sojourns in celestial cities or in the belly of beasts; experiences of death and rebirth; memories of past lives; and trips through regions reminiscent of the Bardo states (intermediate places of the soul's sojourn between incarnations) described in *The Tibetan Book of the Dead*.

It is remarkable that people of different cultures, beliefs and personal histories report similar visions, whether these are induced by psychosis, psychedelic drugs, sudden discharges of the body's subtle energy or *kundalini*, controlled breathing techniques, trance states or religious ecstasies following fasting, prayer, contemplation, meditation or vision questing. In *Beyond Death,* Stanislav Grof comments:

> Confrontation with death is just one aspect of the psyche-
> delic experience. A second important aspect is the struggle
> to be reborn, conceptualized by many subjects as the reliv-
> ing of their birth trauma. In the death-rebirth process,
> dying, being born and giving birth are intimately inter-
> woven. Sequences of extreme emotional and physical suffer-
> ing are followed by experiences of liberation, birth or

rebirth, with visions of brilliant white or golden light (p. 26).

Grof's research into the four stages of birth experienced in controlled psychedelic research bears striking parallels to mythological motifs that refer to the process of soul growth. A much fuller description of these stages and other archetypal experiences elicited not only by psychedelics but by a breathing process that Grof and his wife and colleague, Christina Grof, call Holotropic Breathwork™, can be found in Stanislav Grof's *The Adventure of Self-Discovery.* In brief, the four stages of the birth process elicited by the controlled use of LSD in research settings are these:

Stage 1: Cosmic Engulfment. Grof's research subjects relate this stage to the actual, physical onset of the biological birth process and our cellular memories of that event. In psychedelic sessions this stage is typfied by overwhelming anxiety without being able to pinpoint an exact cause. There is an accompanying tendency to interpret one's surroundings in paranoid terms. If the anxiety mounts, it is often followed by images of being sucked into a whirlpool or swallowed by a huge or frightening beast, as in the story of Jonah in the belly of the whale.

Stage 2: No Exit. This stage is described as corresponding to the part of the birth process when uterine contractions begin but the cervix is still closed. Claustrophobia and visions of torture and physical agony abound here. The person feels victimized and trapped. Worse, there seems to be no hope, no exit from a situation that appears both brutal and meaningless. Grof says that many psychedelic subjects have independently compared this stage to being in hell.

Stage 3: The Death-rebirth Struggle. This stage is described as corresponding to that part of the birth process when the cervix opens. It involves being propelled through the birth canal. Associated images are apocalyptic in scale—wars, natural disasters, huge cataclysms of energy that can also be sexual in nature. Agony and ecstasy coexist, often in the form of battles between good and evil. This stage is marked by hope and the realization that suffering has a definite purpose.

Stage 4: Death and Rebirth. The fourth stage corresponds to the physical process of expulsion from the birth canal, the cutting of the cord and birth as an independent entity. Here suffering and agony lead to complete annihilation of what was, a total ego-death. Following the struggle there are visions of blinding, magnificent light. In Grof's words. "The universe is perceived as indescribably beautiful and radiant; subjects feel themselves cleansed and purged, and speak of redemption, salvation, *moksha*, or *samadhi*."

The stages of psychedelic experience that Grof's research subjects relate to physical birth are directly relevant to the healing of trauma, which, like the physical birth process, is stamped into the memories of our cells. I was enormously excited when I first discovered these stages because they gave me a new framework into which many of my experiences, professional as well as personal, fit.

Rather than viewing fear through the lens of pathology, it can be viewed as a stage in a journey marked by a continuum of death and birth experiences. These experiences relate not only to our physical and psychological history, but also to our soul history, as we'll discuss in the next two chapters when we investigate seeming experiences of reincarnation and the use of past-life therapy to treat fears that are resistant to more conventional approaches.

Having had a psychotic experience of intense fear as a ten-year-old child, I found Grof's research personally relevant. After reading it I was convinced that my experience was not a descent into meaningless madness but an initiatory experience that was a stop along the hero's journey, a Story of soul growth and an instance of what the Grofs call spiritual emergence. Christina Grof has written of her own spontaneous and often frightening experiences of spiritual emergence, experiences that can indeed be difficult to distinguish from psychosis.

In this context I particularly recommend *The Stormy Search for the Self*, by Christina and Stanislav Grof, and *Spiritual Emergency: When Personal Transformation Becomes a Crisis*. The second book, edited by the Grofs, contains contributions from noted psychologists and spiritual teachers that are extremely helpful in putting fear experiences into perspective and determining when psychiatric help is necessary and what kind of help is most likely to aid transformation rather than abort it. This information is also critical as background for understanding methods of healing and transforming trauma that are used in societies other than our own.

THE TREATMENT OF TRAUMA BY RECLAIMING THE SOUL

When a major earthquake hit in Mexico in 1985 many people watched family and friends die before their eyes and subsequently developed PTSD. While medication and psychotherapy were either not helpful or unavailable to these people, public television carried a documentary about a local healer—a Mexican housewife—who could cure PTSD. Like many indigenous shamans, this woman believed that PTSD resulted from loss of the soul. While the person's body was still alive, the soul had been frightened off and must be retrieved from the dark waters of the unconscious, the shamanic underworld.

In order to bring the soul back, the healer knew that she must reawaken the person's dead emotions and help them to relive the trauma. After helping the person into a deeply relaxed state, the woman and her helpers suddenly emitted blood-curdling shrieks and threw buckets of ice on the startled patient. The sudden shock reawakened emotion, and the soul was then retrieved through the reliving of the trauma, while the patient was held and comforted so that he or she could rebond to the world of the living.

Shamans from aboriginal, some Native American, Alaskan and Siberian cultures take "trips" into the underworld with the help of rhythmic chants and drumming—perhaps the world that Grof's LSD patients travel to with chemical help—and retrieve the lost souls of their physically or psychologically sick patients. Unfortunately, since modern psychologists and psychiatrists no longer think in terms of the soul (even though the word "psychology" means the study of the soul), this kind of deep, archetypal healing doesn't usually take place in the modern consulting room.

Whether we are discussing PTSD or the sociopathy that can result from the childhood deprivation of love and subsequent inability to bond with and identify with other human beings, we are indeed discussing soul sickness if not soul loss. The human soul grows through love and connectedness. Perhaps when it is lost or walled off, some of the powerful rituals of soul mending and retrieval used by "primitive" shamans can be successfully adapted to reclaim it. Modern psychologists who are largely unskilled in techniques for reaching the deep unconscious might be aided substantially by studying rituals, psychedelic research and transpersonal forms of healing involving the help of entities from the Other Side, which we will discuss in the next two chapters.

Healing from trauma seems to require at least two crucial elements: reliving the experience and transformation of the trauma. It is the step of transformation that we need to know more about. In the case of the earthquake victims, the transforming element seems to have been love that allowed a rebonding with humanity. A stunning account that gives further insight into the nature of transformation was published in the remarkable book *Shivitti: A Vision.* Billed as "the haunting testimony of a man who had the courage to face a nightmare twice," it is a brilliant account of the therapy of a survivor of Auschwitz who had suffered from PTSD for thirty years before he found treatment for his terrible psychic wounds.

Its author is Ka-Tzetnik 135633 (referring to his *Konzentration Zenter* number from Auschwitz), an Israeli whose Holocaust experience propelled him on a journey of modern-day soul searching that finally led him to the Dutch clinic of Professor Jan C. Bastiaans. Bastiaans is the psychiatrist who first recognized concentration-camp syndrome, successfully treating many camp survivors and other victims of violence with a fascinating therapy involving LSD at his clinic in Leiden.

Because of the exceptional clarity on the part of both physician and patient that is demonstrated in the text of *Shivitti,* I will summarize the treatment and transformation of the trauma in some detail. *Shivitti* is also rich in archetypal Stories, as you will appreciate from the poem that introduces one of the LSD sessions of Ka-Tzetnik 135633's therapy.

A BIRD CALLED THE PHOENIX—
TRANSFORMATION OF A TRAUMA

> A Bird called the Phoenix,
> one thousand years it lives,
> and at the end of those thousand years,
> its nest is engulfed in flames, and consumes it.
> But the germ of its essence survives
> and renews itself and lives.
>
> Midrash Rabbah, Genesis, 19:5

So starts Gate Four, the introduction to the fourth of five LSD therapy sessions described in *Shivitti*.

At first the author/patient was reluctant even to seek treatment for the perpetual psychological hell he had lived in for thirty years following his liberation from Auschwitz. In the foreword to *Shivitti*, he shares his thoughts about seeing Professor Bastiaans and his guilt for beginning treatment:

> Auschwitz is another planet, while we humankind, occupants of planet Earth, have no key to decipher the code name Auschwitz. How dare I commit sacrilege by trifling with those eyes on their way to the crematorium? They knew where they were going. I knew where they were going. The eyes of the one crossing over boring into the eyes of the one remaining behind. The sky silent overhead, the earth silent underfoot. Only a meeting of the eyes and a last silence, the inaudible tread of their feet. For naked and barefoot they went to the crematorium.
>
> For two long years they trod through me, their eyes penetrating mine. And time there, on planet Auschwitz, was not like time here. Each moment there revolved around the cogwheels of a different time-sphere.
>
> Hell-years last longer than light-years.
>
> They left me behind with their gaze sunk in mine. Wouldn't it be a desecration of that silent gaze if I delivered

it up to Prof. Bastiaans at the Psychiatric Department in Leiden? (p. x–xi).

With these poignant reservations, Ka-Tzetnik 135633, a man by the name of Yehiel De-Nur, went for help. Under the influence of five LSD sessions he relived traumas so terrible that, at times, I couldn't have stood to read the descriptions were it not for the transformative vision of *Shivitti* that he had during his first session. *Shivitti* is the eighth verse of the Sixteenth Psalm of David, "I have set the Lord always before me." Central to the vision of these words in Hebrew is the tetragrammaton, YHWH, the four letters that form the mystical, unpronounceable name of the Lord. De-Nur sees these letters, glowing with otherwordly light, dominating the Auschwitz horizon and blotting out the terror.

As De-Nur began reliving his Auschwitz traumas under LSD, he remembered protecting a saintly rabbi from the clubs of the guards as they were herded onto a truck bound for the crematorium. In the LSD vision he asked the rabbi *"Why?"* as the truck was loaded with *mussulmen* (inmates whose skin was all that held their withered bones together). The rabbi told him, "Because it was so decreed." When De-Nur asked by whom it was decreed, the rabbi told him to ask God. As De-Nur lifted his eyes to the heavens in search of God, he saw a riveting, transcendent vision of *shivitti* suspended in magnificence over the horizon. It was aflame in the Auschwitz sky, like a torch, glowing with the colors of the rainbow.

Central to the vision was the holy, unpronounceable name of God, YHWH (sometimes erroneously anglicized to the word Jehovah by Christians). The tetragrammaton glowed with divine light and twin lions guarded its holiness. The lions' faces were human and they were winged, their wings merging with the holy letters. Face to face with this marvelous vision, De-Nur cried out the primeval question of the tortured, perplexed heart in the darkest night of the soul: "God! God! Who decreed?! Who decreed?! Auschwitz—whose is it?"

As he lifted his eyes to God, he saw instead the face of the S.S. man who was loading the truck bound for the ovens. He was a tired man, sleepy, chillingly ordinary, wishing he were home in bed rather than standing in this surreal holocaust in the small hours of a cold, dark morning. De-Nur pondered the S.S. man as he relived the horror of being driven to his impending death in the infamous ovens that belched the stench of burning flesh and bone over miles of Polish countryside:

> Do I hate him? I don't even know his name, just as I don't know the names of the rest of us now being delivered to the crematorium. All at once an additional horror seizes me, one I've not yet known: if this is so, then he could have been standing here in my place, a naked skeleton in this truck, while I, I could have been standing there instead of him, on just such a cold morning doing my job delivering him and millions like him to the crematorium (p. 10).

This thought brought De-Nur to a meeting with his own dark side, the hidden side of us all that we are usually too fearful and horrified even to consider. He writes,

> Oh, Lord, merciful and compassionate Lord, am I the one, the one who's created Auschwitz? It's much worse than that he—the German facing me with the death's skull insignia on his cap, his hands deep in his pockets of his black S.S. coat—could have been in my place. It's that I—and this is the paralyzing horror—I could have been there in his place!
>
> Oh Lord, Lord of Auschwitz heavens, illumine my ignorance of your handiwork, so that I might know who is the being within me now delivered to the crematorium—and why? And who is the being within him delivering me to the crematorium—and why? For you know that at this moment the two of us, dispatcher and dispatched, are equal sons of man, both created by you, in your image (p. 11).

This vision was so profoundly disturbing to De-Nur that it constituted a second trauma, an event not lost on the perceptive Dr. Bastiaans, who encouraged him to face it, dive into it, unravel it while it was still fresh. At first De-Nur could not. Even when he had been asked to testify at the Eichmann trial he had begged not to; simply hearing the word Auschwitz had been too much to take. When he had tried to testify despite his fears he collapsed to the floor in a state of semiparalysis, his face terribly distorted, and had to be hospitalized. The courage it took to relive the trauma under LSD therapy, and then to verbalize his experience to Professor Bastiaans took De-Nur some time to mobilize. Bastiaans, however, believed that De-Nur's "incapacity to give words to your experience is at the root of your soul's torment."

Despite his terror, De-Nur trusted Bastiaans and very slowly continued the LSD sessions and the halting description of the unspeakable horrors he had witnessed and experienced. De-Nur was, in fact, delivered to the ovens in the truck loaded by the S.S. officer referred to in his first session, but by sheer force of will he held onto the side of the truck and found refuge in its coalbin, hiding inside it and escaping later when the truck was brought back to the garage. Bastiaans recognized the pivotal significance of the coalbin as a transformative element for De-Nur's terrible trauma, not by hearing of it firsthand from his patient but by reading about it in the curiously detached third-person description that characterized the books De-Nur had previously written about his Holocaust experiences. As Bastiaans wrote:

> Your act of emerging from that coalbin imprinted your every cell with the consciousness that you were then and there being born: in fact, an infant fully gestated and now leaving darkness for the light of day. At that moment, the instant of exit, your soul proceeded to split. On an organic level you knew that you had left the darkness of that coalbin to be reborn. With the coming of liberation you accepted it. Of necessity, as a natural inevitable result, your irrevocable vow not to abandon the man-born-of-coalbin evolved from organic knowledge. In other words, the name De-Nur is proscribed from appearing as author on those books of testimony. In your own eyes, you would be not only a charlatan, but a grave robber, stealing sacred objects from a tomb accursed by the gods. And right here is your opportunity to discover the answers to all my questions. If you

enter this coalbin, the womb of your rebirth, as into your
soul, you'll find the answers waiting (pp. 66–67).

Bastiaans's statement that, at the moment of exit from the coalbin,
De-Nur's soul had split is at the heart of mending and recovering the
soul after trauma. This survivor never published his books under the
name De-Nur but as Ka-Tzetnik 135633. There was the split. Before
Shivitti De-Nur wrote only in the third person, even when it was
difficult to twist the prose to fit his need to distance himself from
his own experience. After the sessions with Bastiaans, De-Nur was
surprised to find that, without consciously realizing it, he had begun
to write in the first person. He was owning his trauma, mending the
split in his soul. As he did this, the content of his LSD visions changed
and, instead of staying stuck in the birth canal of transformation, he
went through the entire progression of soul birth and rebirth described by Grof.

Liberated from the belly of the beast and the hell of no exit, De-
Nur began to see the Light more frequently, superimposed on the
unspeakable terrors of Auschwitz. Concerning part of the fourth
session he wrote:

> A perfect peace wafts down on me from on high as I repay
> my obligations, one and all. I throw off all the yokes that
> bear down on my neck. I surrender my body to the earth
> and my breath to my Creator, while an ineffable light fills
> me. I haven't known this light since my soul left the man-
> sion of souls, an abode under the throne of Shekhina (the
> divine feminine). I see my soul turn its face toward the
> source of the light. And all my obligations are repaid, every
> one (p. 85).

In the final session, De-Nur poignantly becomes one with his naked
mother as she goes to be gassed. He dies with her in the "showers"
and burns with her body in the crematorium. He then expects to see
the souls of his dead brother and sister along with that of his mother
rising from the infernal chimneys, but instead he sees himself. He
catches up with his mother as she stands before God's throne flanked

by his brother and sister, challenging God with the kind of heart-breaking accusations we heard Job mutter back in Chapter One. De-Nur becomes at once the souls who were burned and the burner, as God is both creator and destroyer. Reliving the moment when he exited the truck, emerging like a black wraith from the coalbin, he remembers shrieking at the surprised S.S. men, "I'm a human being! No evil spirit! No demon! I am human and I want to live!"

De-Nur then escaped into the snowy forest. In his LSD vision he crept back to the pile of corpses in the camp, vowing to be their voice, which he certainly has been. The description of his LSD therapy ends with this stunning scene of transformation, incorporating elements of both a death/rebirth archetype and a near-death experience:

> All the death-riddled skeletons in the pile burst into a single flame that curls into a chariot of fire. I, a mussulman, a skeleton that grows wings; a flaming salamandra (a spirit in Greek mythology who lives in fire for seven years and then resurrects itself), a phoenix raised from my own fire. Like a missile bound for the upper spheres, I shoot up from the launching pad of skeletons into the tempest of my own cry of passion—
>
> And re-enter my body.

In De-Nur's description one recognizes that God is not absent from this holocaust, after all. The divine is present, but the responsibility for Auschwitz is that of humankind. It's up to us, not up to God. The choice between good and evil is a human choice, and the capacity for good and evil, as De-Nur discovered in his identification with the S.S. guard in the first vision, is the choice each of us must make. In our own lives, as well, we can choose to die in the fire of our pains and traumas or to resurrect ourselves like the mythological phoenix. The latter course requires the courage to face old pain with total, complete and naked honesty.

It is likely that the next decade will witness the emergence of new forms of therapy that can help those of us who are still prisoners of trauma to take off from the launching pad of our pain and to heal our souls, as De-Nur did with the help of an exceptional therapist.

Whether or not therapy with LSD is ultimately legalized once more in the United States, it is a powerful drug with the potential to do as much harm as good in all but the most skilled of hands. For that reason, I absolutely counsel against its use other than in clinical situations where it is legally sanctioned and administered by experts. Other methods of inducing similar states, such as the Holotropic Breathwork™ developed by the Grofs, may well prove to have widespread utility in healing from trauma and recovering the soul.

The remarkable therapy of Yehiel De-Nur demonstrates how, with skilled assistance, even the most fearful traumas can often be healed. Yet there are cases in which all attempts to heal fear fail. In some of these instances the fear seems to stem not from traumatic experiences in this life, but from traumas and unresolved situations that appear to have been carried in our unconscious from other lives. In the next two chapters we will delve into the nature of what seem to be memories that span space and time, whether these memories are real or archetypal, and explore how we can change the ending of these old stories to set ourselves free.

CHAPTER SIX

Healing Fear Across Space and Time

Let your hook be always cast; in the pool where you least expect it, there will be a fish.

Ovid

The baggage check-in line was long. By the time I had maneuvered my suitcase through the maze of hassled travelers and presented my documents to the ticket agent I was bored and weary. She, by contrast, was bright-eyed and unusually pleasant for such a busy person. "Are you traveling with a companion on the return trip?" she inquired.

"No, I'll be alone. Why do you ask?" She explained that I had been assigned a middle seat and unless I was traveling with another person I would be more comfortable in an aisle or window seat. I thanked her for being so kind, especially in light of the long line of travelers queued up in back of me. As her deft fingers moved over the computer keyboard, punching up a new boarding pass, she gave me a conspiratorial look and smiled.

"If I wasn't kind I'd hear about it from my spirit guides." Interesting conversation for a ticket agent on the job. Her remark hung pregnant in the air. Should I let it go or follow it up? After all, there was a long line. I decided to take the bait.

"Spirit guides? How do you contact your spirit guides? Through meditation?"

"Oh no." She smiled, stapling my new boarding pass to the ticket. "I'm psychic. My mother is psychic, too. I've been in communication with them for as long as I can remember. But we all have spirit guides." She began making out the tags for my luggage. "Yours are standing behind you right now. Can you feel them?" I shrugged a quick no, wondering if this conversation was some kind of a joke and beginning to feel a little foolish.

"They are telling me about the car accident you had last year, showing me your face all wrapped in bandages. You really did some job on that nose," she said, looking directly into my eyes. She then shook her head and clucked a sound of compassionate knowing.

An eerie feeling came over me as she continued to recount the kind of specific details about the accident that no one could possibly have known. In my heart of hearts I knew that I had not fully reaped the lessons from that accident. Although it had certainly led me to take stock of my life and to make some long overdue changes such as leaving academia, there were some things about it that I still didn't want to face. The accident had come at the end of a terribly dark night of the soul, one that had rivaled my childhood obsessive-compulsive neurosis in terms of the shear starkness of the terror I had experienced.

The cause for that terribly dark night was not, on the surface, the stuff out of which nightmares are made. The triggering event was my inadvertent failure to appropriately credit the work of a colleague in my first book. Although we worked through the difficulty well together, the incident seemed to uncork an ancient bottle out of which the dark genie of primitive fear issued forth—the fear that I was a horribly bad, unworthy human being. After all, if I could hurt someone unconsciously, do something wrong without even realizing it, I reasoned that I could not trust myself. I felt as though all my desires to live a kind and generous life—to care—were a fraud.

I felt profoundly isolated from myself, from others and from the universe for several months after the episode. It was like experiencing hell on earth. This powerful dark night drove me back to therapy, and, while I gained some important insights into my character, I was still unable to fathom where such a powerful, deep-rooted fear could have come from. So I finally gave up trying to understand and buried myself even more deeply in my work at the hospital, as if by helping others I could expiate some dark, secret sin that my soul could not or would not disclose. It was at this point that I had my head-on collision with destiny.

The ticket agent, as if divining my painful thoughts, handed back my travel documents with a look of urgency. "Your spirit guides are there to help you. They want you to become conscious of them. Ask for their help. Listen for them in meditation."

I thanked her and was about to turn away when she added, "And one more thing. They are telling me that the key to your problem can be found in a past life."

"How do I get back to that life?" I asked quickly, suspending judgment about whether or not I even believed in past lives. Her instructions were terse.

"Go into meditation," she advised, "and imagine a tunnel. Then tumble down it backward." I tried her suggestion as soon as I settled into my seat on the half-filled DC-10 to Chicago. Nothing much happened. I tried again in my hotel room that night and fell asleep. I tried once or twice more when I got home and then became discouraged. Nonetheless, the airport conversation remained vivid in my mind, and in my body. Little shivers still go up my back when I bring back the mental image of that kindly, maternal ticket agent looking fondly over my shoulder and relaying urgent messages from an unseen world.

COSMIC SECRET AGENTS

The ticket agent was not the only cosmic secret agent that appeared to help me when the time was right. A few months after the "airport connection" I went to a conference of hospital administrators to which I had been invited to give a keynote address about mind/body healing. The evening before the conference our hosts held a reception so that the various presenters could meet one another.

Although we hardly had time to talk, I was particularly drawn to a woman, Magaly Rodriguez Mossman, who does unusual work with imagery. The two kinds of imagery that are commonly used both in psychotherapy and mind/body medicine are called directive and receptive. In *directive imagery* you are guided to think about a particular subject, like relaxing at the beach. In *receptive imagery* you are asked open questions—for example, "Can you remember a time when you felt happy?"—and are then encouraged to receive images from your own unconscious or from some deeper, archetypal store of common wisdom.

Magaly uses another form of imagery, a *transpersonal* form, in which she silently asks a question of the soul of the person she is guiding. She then asks you to consciously note what images come up when she asks a subsequent series of audible questions. At the end of the session she reveals what the initial, silent question was and helps you interpret the images that your soul produced as an answer. Since this technique bypasses the conscious mind—after all, you do not know what question has been posed—there is no chance for you to "think up" the answers. Relatively pure information can therefore be accessed from the unconscious mind through such transpersonal imagery.

The morning that the conference began I met Magaly and Carole Ann, a friend of hers, at the coffee break. They were straightforward and efficient. Carole Ann remarked that she had no idea why she had accompanied Magaly to this conference, other than a strong inner feeling that they were to help someone. I, they had both concurred, was the one. Was there any way they could be of service? "Why, yes," I replied, getting used to having members of the cosmic secret service coalesce out of the mists. "I have this recurrent pattern of terrifying, paranoid fear that I will mistakenly hurt someone. It's haunted me for years and no type of therapy has helped." They smiled and offered to meet me in my room at five o'clock that evening.

They were punctual, and I was soon engaged in a transpersonal imagery session that gave Magaly some clues to what seemed to be a past-life genesis of my fears. Carole Ann, who is highly intuitive, was simultaneously getting impressions of a past life in ancient Egypt in which I had inadvertently caused serious injury to a sister. As a temple priestess, I had brought my sister into the cloister as an initiate, not out of her needs, but out of my own unconscious desire to be powerful. Unprepared for the intensity of the experience, she went mad. I was grief-stricken and could not forgive myself for betraying her needs to serve my own. If this was true and some ancient trauma was recorded in my soul, it was no wonder that a similar incident in which I felt that I had betrayed another person in this life triggered such deep suffering.

My soul was grieving not only for an incident that occurred in this life, but for one or possibly more similar incidents that had occurred in the dim corridors of the past. The unconscious guilt and fear that I would repeat this pattern had made me very wary, always scrutinizing and rescrutinizing every action to see if there was anything I might have done that could be hurtful to someone. When, in spite of this excessive care, I had in fact been unconsciously hurtful to another person, I reacted with a pain that was clearly unreasonable in terms of my current life experience, but extremely reasonable in light of old soul memories.

As Carole Ann revealed some of the details of the lifetime she had seen, again I got little chills of recognition, tingles that I believe are a message from the Higher Self to pay close attention to whatever is happening. My way of paying attention is two-fold. I go inward to listen for the voice of my Higher Self, and I go outward to the library to research themes of interest. In the case of past lives, the "data base" is relatively small, but before we continue the denouement of my own past-life journeys, I want to share some of what I found in my research.

IS REINCARNATION LITERALLY TRUE?

Let me start by summarizing my conclusions. No one can prove it, but I strongly suspect that the answer is yes, no and maybe. While the evidence both for and against reincarnation is inconclusive, the idea certainly appeals to me. And no matter what other explanations can be offered for what seem to be past lives, there is no way to diminish the therapeutic benefit that many people have had from undergoing what seem to be regressions into past lives.

One of the most complete popular accounts of the past-life therapy of a single patient is given by psychiatrist Brian Weiss in his book *Many Lives, Many Masters*. This case is particularly noteworthy because neither Dr. Weiss nor his patient believed in past lives or were thinking about them when he hypnotically regressed her in order to unearth the possible traumatic roots of several resistant phobias. Rather than leading to traumas in this life, however, the regression led to a series of traumas in what appeared to be past lives. With the help of spirit guides that spoke through his patient when she reached the moment of death and came into the Light, the traumas were resolved and the phobias disappeared.

I was particularly fascinated with Dr. Weiss's experiences because of the courage he showed in publishing information that is completely at odds with his scientific orientation. His own training was in biological psychiatry (the use of drugs) and he was chairman of the Department of Psychiatry at the Mount Sinai Medical Center in Miami when cases of the reincarnation type suddenly began appearing in his practice. As I tour the country giving workshops and speaking with therapists I have heard countless stories reminiscent of Dr. Weiss's. Many therapists who have never considered, or are even antagonistic to, the idea of past lives stumble onto what appear to be past-life memories while using hypnotic regression, deep relaxation or visualization with their patients. In some cases the past life memories first come up in patients' dreams.

Since traditionally schooled therapists are not trained to consider past lives as a possible source of their patients' problems, such experiences are often shocking to the therapist, who must then seek peer support and supervision to deal with an area beyond his or her expertise.

A number of fascinating case histories of the therapeutic use of past-life regression are presented in Jungian analyst Roger Woolger's scholarly, fascinating book *Other Lives, Other Selves*. Whenever a patient shows repetitive behavior that is hard to influence, or as in my case, has a particular fear that is resistant to traditional modes of therapy, past-life regression may be of benefit, regardless of whether either the patient or the therapist believes that what is being recalled are actually past lives. Woolger makes the point that, regardless of literal truth, there is another kind of truth—psychic truth, which he defines as "that which is real for the patient." He explains to his patients that it doesn't matter if they believe in reincarnation or not because when the unconscious mind is asked in the proper way, it will almost always produce a past-life memory.

But 25 percent of the world's population—largely Hindus and Buddhists—do believe in reincarnation as a doctrine of faith. According to Gallup polls, 28 percent of Americans also believe in reincarnation, despite the fact that the United States is a predominantly Christian country. While scholars are still arguing about whether the early Church taught reincarnation or not, by medieval times reincarnation was a heresy. The current Church dogma is that we get one chance to prove ourselves worthy of an eternity in either heaven or hell. Reincarnationists, on the other hand, posit a self-correcting series of lives governed by the law of karma. The soul is not judged but given the chance for growth; it can constantly gain wisdom through being drawn back into situations where it has "unfinished business." By the end of this process—after it has experienced every action generated through its own free will—it returns to the Light with the wisdom and compassion to be a worthy companion to the Creator.

Believers in reincarnation generally posit several lines of logic to uphold their beliefs. First, if each soul had only one lifetime in which to prove its "worthiness," how could a person born into abuse, poverty, war or neglect possibly be getting an opportunity equal to a person born into more satisfactory circumstances? Second, reincarnation would seem to explain child prodigies with exceptional abilities. Where does a Mozart or an Einstein come from unless their talents were developed in previous lifetimes? Third, reincarnation would explain the "unfairness" of things. Why is one person born into poverty and another into wealth? Why is an innocent bystander shot at the scene of a robbery?

Seen over many incarnations, those things that seem accidental or unfair would instead reveal a perfect logic in the playing out of the law of karma—that is, cause and effect. If we do indeed reap what we sow, then we must ultimately experience every action we have put into motion through our own free will. If we have murdered, we will be drawn back to violence, perhaps as a victim of violence, in order to develop empathy. Or perhaps we will become a great surgeon in order to pay back the Universe for the taking of life by giving life instead. As discussed earlier, it is important not to become a karma fundamentalist who twists all misfortunes into "bad karma." While I believe absolutely in the law of cause and effect, I also believe that the subtleties of the process are well beyond an analysis through simplistic ideas of good and bad.

The commonest argument against reincarnation is that people don't ordinarily remember past lives. The Kabbalists, who are Jewish mystics, explain this fact rather poetically by saying that at the moment of our birth an angel dips us into a potion of forgetfulness. John Van Auken, a long-time student of Edgar Cayce, who was perhaps the best-known psychic of this century, explains our forgetfulness in a more "scientific" way. In his fine book *Born Again and Again*, Van Auken suggests that our conscious mind ceases functioning at death, much as we lose consciousness in sleep. In the fourth- and fifth-dimensional realms in which we function between incarnations, we use what Edgar Cayce called the subconscious mind—the mind we know in dreams, visions and intuitions.

At the time of reincarnation, according to Van Auken, the soul must develop another conscious mind to function in three-dimensional reality. This is different from the mind used in the previous incarnation and different from the subconscious mind we dream with and use in other realities. Therefore it has no memory of previous lives. We can, however, retrieve those memories by using our subconscious mind, which is exactly the way that past-life regressions are accomplished. But are there any instances in which the subconscious mind can spontaneously break through and yield past-life memories whose details can be objectively verified?

Roger Woolger carefully reviewed the work of Dr. Ian Stevenson of the University of Virginia, who has been collecting such "cases of the reincarnation type" since 1960. In the spirit of a good detective, Stevenson has trekked the globe collecting firsthand reports about children from India, Sri Lanka, Turkey and Lebanon who show evidence of recalling past lives. He and his team interview the child, the family and any available witnesses. They have unearthed fascinating cases in which the child is taken to another village and is able to point out his old house, place of business and personal effects.

Critics of Stevenson's work, however, cite the fact that the cases he has researched come from cultures where belief in reincarnation is a matter of faith. This could lead to a bias because of the unconscious desire of the children to please others and thus pick up subtle cues from people who knew the deceased. Nonetheless, such cases are difficult to disprove. The ability to flawlessly pick out belongings from a past life, by the way, is part of the method by which each new Dalai Lama is verifed after certain omens lead wise men to the child. The current Dalai Lama is said to be the fourteenth reincarnation of the Buddha of Compassion.

Woolger himself cites the case of an American man who retrieved a memory of a past life as a landholder in France. Having remembered both his name and date of birth, the man traveled to France and indeed found the birth record of just such an individual. Had the landholder been an important enough person to appear in history books, one could then reason that the name had been retrieved through unconscious recall of a historical fact. But this was apparently not the case.

Detractors of reincarnation often disavow it by claiming that what appears to be past-life recall is in fact based on information learned and forgotten in this life. Knowledge of history, languages and many other facts are stored away on the photographic plate of the unconscious and can be developed and brought to mind under the right circumstances. When people are undergoing brain surgery, for example, detailed memories of events such as a random day in kindergarten can be elicited through stimulation of certain cortical areas. Apparently such insignificant details as the color of the teacher's shoes are stored somewhere in our minds! I do believe that some of what comes up in past-life memories is likely to involve such forgotten knowledge from this life, because in the realm of the unconscious where all memory resides, there is neither time nor space. However, the potential "mixing" of memories from the recent past and more distant past does not invalidate the possibility that some of those memories were recorded in actual past lives.

Another common argument against reincarnation is that too many people claim to have been famous persons in their past lives. This illusion is reinforced by hokey cable-TV ads for "psychics" who are ready and willing to tell you about glamorous past lives for as long as you pay the exorbitant toll on their 900 number. But the idea that there are too many rulers and too few peasants falls away when past-life regressions are done in a serious manner rather than as superficial entertainment and ego boosting.

I certainly don't espouse past-life therapy for everybody. It can be emotionally draining, perilous work to relive a very old trauma in excruciating detail. If such traumas are brought up without being worked through, moreover, they may do more harm than good. If your own inner guidance leads you to an exploration of past lives, find a qualified therapist to help you. Don't try it yourself, and don't rely on well-meaning but unskilled friends.

You may be able to locate past-life therapists in your area through word of mouth or by contacting Dr. Brian Weiss, Dr. Roger Woolger, Dr. Morris Netherton or Dr. Elena Burton, all listed under "Past-Life Therapy" in the Resources section of this book. If you find a therapist who does past-life regressions, put them to the same tests you would any other potential health-care provider. Ask about their training, request references, interview them and then add your intuition to what your research provides. If you have any reservations at all about a person with whom you plan to do a past-life regression, don't do it.

Roger Woolger, as well as several therapists I know who do past-life regression work, maintain that most regressions evoke very ordinary lives and, more to the point, unpleasant and traumatic lives rather than glamorous ones. Furthermore, past lifetimes seem to surface in groups, or clusters, that relate to problems a person is trying to resolve in this life. This is exactly what happened to me.

KARMA CLEANING—
THE HEALING OF MEMORIES

I tried to outmaneuver the next cosmic secret agent who was sent to help me unravel the story of my fear. Her name is Elizabeth

Lawrence, and she is a Mari-El healer. Mari-El is a system for healing old memories without regard for when in time and space they might have occurred. The story of Mari-El is fascinating. A woman by the name of Ethel Lombardi had been a Reiki healer (a system of healing in which the healer acts as a conduit for divine light) for many years. Her own health, however, was failing.

On an airplane to the Mayo Clinic to receive treatment for a failing heart, she experienced a miraculous healing—a spontaneous and complete restoration of her heart to normal—when a rainbow entered the airplane and bathed her in its light. Subsequently, Ms. Lombardi "received" instructions for a new type of healing through a feminine energy that she experienced as Mary, the mother of Jesus. In this system, Mary and her angels are called upon to oversee the healing which consists of drawing out and transforming traumatic memories that are stored in the body's seven subtle energy systems, or chakras. The system is called Mari-El healing (Mari from Mary, and El from Elohim, a Hebrew word for God).

Beth Lawrence is a pastoral counselor with a background in traditional psychotherapy as well as Mari-El healing. She happens to live a few minutes down the street, but I didn't know her until she called one day, hoping to meet me and get together for a talk. She offered me a Mari-El treatment. I was not enthusiastic. Through the years I have had lots of offers to experience different kinds of therapies, and, if they are useful, a Pandora's box of unfinished business usually opens. I was not in the mood to go sorting through Pandora's box at that time, or to pour out my soul to a stranger. I politely declined. But Beth was persistent. Eventually we met for coffee and over time became friends. When a bridge of trust had formed, I agreed to have a Mari-El session.

It made perfect sense to me that old, unhealed memories would be stored in the body and in the body's subtle energy system. Many body-workers have experienced this when they treat a particular part of the body and a flood of emotions, often accompanied by specific memories, erupts. Old grief, for example, is sometimes stored as the proverbial lump in the throat. Before each session Beth would invoke her helpers in the unseen world, the Mari-El angels, and pray for the best possible outcome for me. Then, as I lay comfortably relaxed on the floor, she would focus her attention on my field of subtle energy. Holding her hands above my eyes, for example, she would ask me what I saw. And astonishing memories would come to mind.

Several painful memories from childhood surfaced first. I would tell Beth what came to mind, and she would lead me through a healing of the memory, asking questions about what was happening, having me explain things to and comfort my inner child, and finally bringing me through a forgiveness of the adult who had hurt me. The process was deeply emotional, as real as if it were happening at that very moment. Since there is neither space nor time in the realm of the unconscious, experiences accessed from those memory banks have the same emotional intensity as when they actually occurred.

Over the course of four sessions, clusters of painful memories from this life came up in association with unhealed childhood experiences. With painstaking care Beth evoked the memories, we healed them together, and, with the help of her unseen helpers, she cleared the residue of the memories from my energy body. In effect, we were completing old karma, cleaning it out so that my soul could be free of the compulsion to repeat hurtful experiences.

In Sanskrit the old impressions that we take with us out of this life—the unhealed memories that are storehouses of regrets, resentments and fears—are called *samskaras.* These memories are etched on the plate of our souls. According to Eastern philosophy, the moment of death is the time when these memories become indelibly inscribed. If we go to our deaths with unfinished business, these *samskaras* will stay with us as karma. The need to complete this karma will ineluctably draw us back into similar situations in other times and places, in this world or in others, where we can meet the result of our actions and transcend them in the development of wisdom and compassion.

Between sessions with Beth I had vivid dreams that related to the memories that had come up. Pieces of unfinished business that I had found too shameful to think about begged for expression. After the fourth session, I knew that the time was right to heal some very painful memories, including those that related to my car accident, to the episode that preceded it in which I had felt intensely ashamed at failing to sufficiently credit the work of a colleague and to difficulties I had experienced with a former boss.

During the fifth and final session these memories came up with incredible intensity. Beth was working in the area of my solar plexus, the energy center where self-worth is located, when I suddenly retrieved a memory from an unfamiliar setting. The "bones" of the memory came back during the session. I retrieved the "flesh" subsequently when I entered a relaxed state in meditation, went back to what appeared to be a previous lifetime and experienced entire scenes unfolding in memory about whatever aspect of the lifetime I sought for further information.

In the memory I was a small, plain woman in my mid-twenties in London during a period of religious persecution. I was a midwife, and, like many midwives of the day, I was also a healer and an herbalist. I was in a basement room with a group of women, a hiding place where we were having a meeting. Holding a woven basket and standing off to one side, I felt deeply ashamed and feared chastisement and rejection.

An investigator from the Church had come to my modest rooms and accused me of being a witch. It was clear that he knew most of the midwives in the area and that we were all being rounded up for reformation or execution, depending on how well placed we were in society. I was a poor widow with two small children and no living relatives. If I were killed I feared that the children would become street urchins in the wretched city of London. I knew they would not survive. I was offered clemency if I would testify against the other women I worked with.

The conflict was unbearable. If I testified against them, admitting publicly that we were healers, these good women might be killed as witches. If I did not, my children would surely perish. With terrible anguish I decided to save my children. And with great shame I also realized that I wanted to save myself, that perhaps even without the children I might have made the same decision. The pain of that realization erupted in horrible racking sobs. The guilt, shame and self-hatred I felt in reliving that memory was nearly unbearable, and very familiar. It was exactly the same feeling I had experienced when I inadvertently hurt my colleague.

Beth instructed me to call the two midwives I had betrayed into a bubble of light in my mind. I did so with great trepidation, for my heart was heavy and I felt crippled with the guilt that had hounded me for centuries. With enormous emotion, I told these women exactly how I had felt and why I had testified against them. There was no justification. It was simply the best I could do at that time. I asked for their forgiveness in our vivid mental conversation, and I was amazed at their tenderness. They understood that I had been put in a position where there were no clear choices. They explained that I must understand that the issue was not about betraying them but about self-doubt and self-hatred. I had long ago been forgiven by everyone but myself. I was holding my own soul hostage, and it was time to let go.

These two midwives also told me that the boss with whom I had had such a conflicted relationship was none other than the inquisitor who had first arrested me. He, too, was working out the karma from that lifetime. He, too, needed to understand the circumstance, assume responsibility and then forgive himself. They suggested that we all pray for him. The relief that I experienced in reliving this memory was tremendous, and the immediate result is that the residual resentment I had harbored against the problematic boss melted away. I also got valuable insight about the pattern of paranoid fear that came up whenever I thought I had hurt another person. It was related, at least in part, to the heavy guilt of betraying my sisters in spirit, the midwives.

WHENCE AND WHITHER THE STORIES

The two past-life memories that I had retrieved to that point—one with Beth and one with Magaly and Carole Ann—centered on issues of betrayal. These issues felt deeply familiar, and I wondered if they were actually past-life memories or simply my unconscious weaving stories out of the emotionally charged events of this life. After all, a similar process certainly occurs in dreams. The fact that the stories had profound healing potential was not at issue. My intellect was simply curious about the objective reality of reincarnation. Did my soul actually inhabit the body of that midwife in medieval London? Did I once have a sister in ancient Egypt who went mad when I sought to initiate her into Temple Mysteries before she was prepared? I have no way to answer these questions. But I do have some musings about where these stories come from and how they serve us.

Dr. Fred Alan Wolf is a renowned physicist whose avid interest in the connections between science and states of consciousness has given rise to several books that speculate on the nature of the mind and the Universe. In *The Dreaming Universe,* he cites the work of Henry Corbin, a noted French scholar of Islam, on the "imaginal realm." We enter this realm when we dream, during near-death and other out-of-body experiences, and possibly in those twilight zone experiences like purported UFO abductions that seem absolutely real to the experiencer. The state of consciousness that occurs during hypnosis, meditation, reverie and deep relaxation is a doorway into that realm. In the view of Corbin and others this realm is ontologically real, that is, it has objective reality. Imaginal is not imaginary. On the other hand, imaginal reality is substantially different from our usual waking world.

Shamans enter the imaginal realm on behalf of other souls. According to many shamanic traditions, when we suffer a trauma we lose part of our soul. It stays stuck to the trauma, lost in the imaginal realm beyond space and time. We cannot move on and experience newness in this world because invisible cords keep us tethered to pain and sorrow in another time and place. Many cultures believe that this soul loss is directly responsible for mental and physical illness, a point of view that I share at least in part. It is the shaman's job to enter the imaginal realm and free the part of the soul that is bound.

The imaginal realm in which shamans work is the reality in which past-life regressions take place. This realm is filled with the kind of cross-cultural symbolism that appears in mythology, in the Tarot, in the archetypes that C. G. Jung discussed. These symbols are part of universal stories—First Stories—through which all souls pass on their journey back out of matter to a reunion with the Light. I believe that all of the stories that are retrieved in past-life regressions are real in the imaginal realm of archetypes, but that only some of them once took place in third-dimensional reality.

Here is how the mechanics, or I should say metaphysics, of my theory work. Our culture typically assumes that solid objects are more real than thoughts. This in turn leads to the erroneous assumption that solid matter give rise to thoughts. Yet we have reviewed evidence in prior chapters that consciousness—the thinking, feeling, reflective capacity that we identify as self—both survives the death of the brain and operates across distances quite independently of the brain. Matter is simply a lower vibrational form of thought energy. And energy, as Einstein taught, can be neither created nor destroyed.

The esoteric teachings of ancient cultures view reality as a realm of thought energy from which ideas coalesce and precipitate into the denser world of physical form. In other words, things that are materially real have a prior reality in the imaginal realm. And long after physical existence is over, the actions we performed and the thoughts we created continue to exist as what have been called elementals in the imaginal realm. Third-dimensional reality, in contrast, is a less-enduring level of creation, a phantom world that vanishes like a dream when we wake up at death.

The physical world in which we search for the objective reality of past lives is therefore only a projection of a more enduring reality in which every story ever lived—and many that may not have been physically lived—are recorded and continue to exist eternally. Since all stories have their roots in this realm, I believe that the powerful experiences encountered in past-life regressions are objectively real, whether or not they were ever physically real.

This hypothesis would explain why more than one person can have an emotionally cathartic, deeply healing past-life regression in which they reenact the life of Mary Magdalene, Joan of Arc or some other figure of mythic proportions. These lifetimes are archetypes—master stories—that exist forever in imaginal reality and that every one of us lives through in some variation sometime in the evolution of our souls.

In the course of growing our souls into what John Van Auken calls companions to God we must face the temptations to misuse our free will, master the different realms of consciousness and choose to align our personal will with divine will as co-creators. In completing this panoramic jigsaw puzzle of soul growth, we eventually experience all the archetypes: lover and beloved, betrayer and betrayed, parent and child, victim and oppressor, the wise one and the fool, teacher and learner, saint and sinner.

BEYOND DUALITY— FREEING THE STUCK SOUL

Our soul gets stuck, however, when we stay caught in one of the stories and fail to finish our business and move on. This is when a modern-day shamanic soul rescue—a past-life regression—can make us conscious of how we got stuck in a repeating rut and give us the tools to get out.

Third-dimensional reality is projected from higher dimensions by splitting wholeness into opposites: male and female, right and left, night and day, good and evil, above and below, me and you, human and divine. And, to bring the discussion back to where I was stuck in my own past-life regressions, betrayer and betrayed. Identifying with either one of these opposites leads to the same outcome— staying stuck.

One of my favorite poems is called "The Thunder, Perfect Mind." It is a poem about embodying the opposites that was accidentally unearthed by a farmer in the Egyptian desert town of Nag Hammadi in 1945 and preserved in a large earthenware jar with fifty-one other ancient manuscripts. These precious parchments were buried nearly 1,800 years ago by monks who feared their destruction by the early Church. You can read about the Nag Hammadi manuscripts in the widely acclaimed book of theologian Elaine Pagels, *The Gnostic Gospels*. Or you can read the original manuscripts, published in a single volume called *The Nag Hammadi Library*.

"The Thunder, Perfect Mind" is a long poem from *The Nag Hammadi Library* written in the voice of an ancient feminine wisdom who states that she was sent forth from "the power." She admonishes us not to be ignorant of her anywhere or anytime, but to be on our guard. Her enigmatic poem is a warning not to get stuck in duality. Seven pages long, it is comprised of paradoxes:

> For I am the first and the last.
> I am the honored one and the scorned one.
> I am the whore and the holy one.
> I am the wife and the virgin.
> For I am knowledge and ignorance.
> I am shame and boldness.
> I am shameless: I am ashamed.
> I am strength and I am fear.
> I am war and I am peace.
> Give heed to me.
> I am the one who is disgraced and the great one.

The apocryphal Acts of John sum up a similar teaching of Jesus, which was said to be a hymn that he sang to his disciples at the Last Supper. Here are a few of the verses:

> I would be saved, and I would save. Amen.
> I would be wounded, and I would wound. Amen.
> I would eat, and I would be eaten. Amen.
> Whoso danceth not, knoweth not what cometh to pass. Amen.

To know wholeness we must dance the opposites. I learned this universal principle at a very personal level as the saga of my past-life memories continued to unfold over the months that followed. Only when I could hold the position both of betrayer and betrayed—with a willingness both to forgive and be forgiven—could I transcend that particular duality. Holding onto these or any opposites, on the other hand, feeds karmic loops that recreate dark nights of the soul endlessly across space and time.

CHAPTER SEVEN

Forgiveness and Freedom— The Telling of an Ancient Tale

Since then, at an uncertain hour,
That agony returns
And till my ghastly tale is told,
This heart within me burns.

Samuel Taylor Coleridge, The Rime of the Ancient Mariner*

One evening when our son Justin was about six, I paraphrased Jesus' Sermon on the Mount to him from the Gospel of Matthew. I apologized when we were finished, assuming that it might have been boring, and promised to buy him a picture-book Bible. Justin was sitting on my lap with his head resting against my shoulder. He was so still that I thought he might have drifted off to sleep. As I apologized, he turned around and looked into my eyes, "Why would you want to buy me a picture book?" he asked. He continued matter-of-factly, "I see all the pictures in my head. After all, I was there. I lived

---

*When I read this excerpt from *The Rime of the Ancient Mariner* in *Other Lives, Other Selves*, by Dr. Roger Woolger, it spoke perfectly to the unbidden repetitions of my own fears, whose roots went back to an ancient tale that had to be told in order for me to find peace.

other men in the desert. It was hot in the day and cold ... 'e didn't eat much and we waited for a great teacher." ...nt on in some detail, describing the life of an Essene (John the Baptist was one of these mystic, ascetic Jews). With great reverence he talked of being in the crowd on the day that Jesus gave the sermon I had just read, but he said that the sermon was not actually given on a mountain but on a flat area. It is interesting that a similar discourse in the Gospel of Luke is called the Sermon on the Plain. Furthermore, Justin continued, grabbing his blanket and settling back into my lap, I had left out some of the best parts about how Jesus taught that we should be kind to each other.

As Justin grew older, the veil between this world and the other thickened, as it does for us all. Aside from an extraordinarily compassionate nature, he is no more mystical than most of us. But until the age of about eight he would quite readily discuss his visions of God, the presence of his deceased grandfather, what it was like to sit in the lap of Jesus and other topics that seemed absolutely astounding coming literally from the mouth of a babe.

Intrigued by Justin's comments about how I had left out the best parts of the Sermon on the Mount—or, as he would have preferred to call it, the Sermon on the Plain—I scoured these beautiful scriptures. Among other topics, Jesus' powerful teaching gives a concise statement about how forgiveness ends the repetitive cycles put into motion by the law of karma. In Matthew 4:17 Jesus states, "For truly, I say to you, till heaven and earth pass away, not an iota, not a dot, will pass from the law until all is accomplished." The sermon proceeds to tell us how all is to be accomplished, in other words, how we are to transcend our karma.

Jesus says that in the old law (the law of Moses given in the Ten Commandments) we were told not to kill, but that is not enough to enter the Kingdom of Heaven. We must let go of our anger and resentments, as well as seek forgiveness from those we hurt. "So if you are offering your gift at the altar, and there remember that your brother had something against you, leave your gift there before the altar and go; first be reconciled to your brother, and then come and offer your gift," or you will "be put in prison; truly, I say to you, you will never get out till you have paid the last penny" (Matthew 5:23–24, 26).

The way the penny is paid and the karmic cycle is ended is through forgiveness—of ourselves, of others, and of God, against whom we may have railed about the apparent unfairness of our trials and our suffering. In the Sermon on the Mount, Jesus gave what came to be called the Lord's Prayer as a daily practice of forgiveness. Unfortunately, the poor translations of Jesus' original Aramaic words into Greek and then into English obscured some of the richness of his teachings. Compare the King James Version of the Lord's Prayer to the far more sensitive and factual excerpts from the translation by Neil Douglas-Klotz from *Prayers of the Cosmos: Meditations on the Aramaic Words of Jesus:*

> Pray then like this:
> Our Father which art in heaven. [O Birther!
>   Father-Mother of the Cosmos.]
> Hallowed be thy name.
> Thy Kingdom come.
> Thy will be done, on earth as it is in heaven.
> Give us this day our daily bread. [Grant what we
>   need each day in bread and insight.]
> And forgive us our debts, as we forgive our debtors.
>   [Loose the cords of mistakes binding us, as we
>   release the strands we hold of other's guilt.]
> And lead us not into temptation, but deliver us
>   from evil. [Do not let surface things delude us,
>   but free us from what holds us back.]
> For thine is the kingdom, and the power, and the
>   glory, forever.
> Amen.
>
>   (Matthew 6:9–13, King James Version)

Both translations of Jesus' words stress the importance of forgiveness. In the commentary that accompanies Douglas-Klotz's magnificent translation, he gives several possible meanings of the Aramaic

word *washboqlan,* which is usually rendered as "forgiveness." "Recip-
rocally absorb," "return to its original state," "embrace with emptiness" and "reestablish slender ties to" give the reader a better idea
of the kind of letting go and unraveling of old knots that Jesus had
in mind as he prayed. Likewise the word traditionally translated as
"debts" can be rendered as "hidden past," "secret debt" or "any 'inner
fruit' that affects the intelligence and the soul negatively."

RETHINKING FORGIVENESS

These understandings of forgiveness radiate the kind of gentle
depth and kindness that Justin believes he heard from Jesus 2,000
years ago. The rich sound of the Aramaic words registers in the body,
bringing forth the very emotions that are conveyed more weakly in
translation. I highly recommend the meditations in *Prayers of the
Cosmos,* which use the original Aramaic sounds as focuses for body-
centered meditation. Forgiveness, a profound state of letting go, is
experienced as the freedom of deep relaxation and comfort in the
body.

Mental concepts of forgiveness are less immediate than the physical
act of letting go and are often confused and confusing. Forgiveness
is not the misguided act of condoning irresponsible, hurtful behavior.
Nor is it a superficial turning of the other cheek that leaves us feeling
victimized and martyred. Rather it is the finishing of old business
that allows us to experience the present, free of contamination from
the past.

Applied to ourselves, forgiveness requires a thorough consideration
of any hurtful acts we may have consciously or unconsciously committed, coupled with any necessary restitution. In the process—
which I discuss at length in *Guilt Is the Teacher, Love Is the Lesson*—
we learn about responsibility, sensitivity, empathy and kindness.
These learnings are internalized, and the process is complete, when
we forgive ourselves by losing our attachment to what we have done
and celebrating instead what we have become.

Applied to other people, forgiveness is a process through which we
seek to free ourselves from the bondage to another person that is

maintained for as long as we stand in judgment of them. While anger is an appropriate initial response to hurt, it is crippling if we continue to use it to make ourselves right by making another person wrong. Sometimes we choose to hold onto anger at someone who is dead, as if that anger will show them a thing or two! Or perhaps we cherish our anger in the mistaken belief that it makes us more powerful and less of a victim. But in this case we become the victims of our own anger, which weakens us rather than leading to authentic empowerment.

I once did a kinesiology, or muscle strength, demonstration with a group of teenagers at a school for delinquent children. Many of the boys were inner-city gang members, and a metal detector at the door was the only thing that kept guns and knives out of the classroom. When I asked the boys which they thought made them more powerful, love or anger, they responded with studied looks of boredom, disgust and a few snickers.

I asked for a volunteer who would help me decide the issue. At first I thought that no one would come up, but one young man finally joined me in front of his peers. I asked him to hold his strongest arm straight out from the shoulder and resist my efforts to push it down. I was amazed at how weak he was—he could hardly resist the vertical force of my little arm (I am barely 5 feet, 4 inches tall and a size 6) pushing down on his.

I had done this demonstration before at workshops with small women who had much more arm strength than this muscular teen whose lifeforce had already been sapped by rage. I then asked him to gather all his power by thinking hard about something that really made him mad. He closed his eyes for a moment and then nodded when he was ready. I was able to collapse his arm with the pressure of two fingers! The glare on his face gave way to a look of surprise. I then asked him to think of something that he loved and retested his arm. His original strength—or I should say weakness—had returned. Perhaps if this unfortunate youngster had been able to access a truly loving memory the demonstration would have worked as usual. He would have been as strong as steel when he tuned into the power of love.

If a boy like this wrestled you to the sidewalk and made off with your wallet, you would probably be angry at first, and your anger might serve you well. Perhaps it would warn you not to walk alone in certain parts of the city or encourage you to take a course in self-defense. If your anger turned to empathy it might lead you to join a big-brother or big-sister program or to champion the disadvantaged. But if you held onto your anger it would eventually turn into a liability. Perhaps it would ferment into prejudice, an attitude of victimization or a desire for revenge. These attitudes would erode your peace of mind and weaken you physically and emotionally. Spiritually your anger would create karmic ties to similar situations in the future.

Whether or not we forgive the teenage thief—which amounts to choosing bondage or freedom for ourselves—he is ultimately responsible for his own actions. Our decision to hold onto our anger and self-righteousness or to let them go is not a message to God about another person's guilt or innocence. We are not the judge and God is not the jury. Each of us holds the keys to our own destiny.

For me, the unraveling of a third past-life memory provided the keys to self-forgiveness and the forgiveness of others that finally allowed me to open a new door in my life and find freedom from the lifelong terror of being hurtful to others.

GATEWAY TO FREEDOM

The gateway to freedom began to surface spontaneously during the Jewish high holy days of 1991. While I am not an observant Jew per se, I try to observe holidays (read: holy days) from all traditions that recur cyclically each year and provide windows of opportunity to come closer to God. These holidays include times for sowing and reaping, for joyful thanksgiving and silent communion. There are times to celebrate the dying away of the old and the birth of new Light within.

The Jewish high holy days span a ten-day period between Rosh Hashana (the New Year) and Yom Kippur (the Day of Atonement). Archetypally, the Jewish high holy days are a period of grace during which all past karma can be cleared away. From both a practical and traditional standpoint, they are days of reflection and repentance. One reviews the past year and does anything necessary to come to peace with it. The soul is cleansed as one takes responsibility for one's actions, making any restitution that might be called for and asking forgiveness from oneself, other people and God. One likewise grants forgiveness to others and receives forgiveness from God.

I was meditating one morning during this time when the ancient Jews believed (although many modern Jews have forgotten these beliefs) that the gates of heaven are open. As part of my usual preparatory routine before deep, silent meditation, I waited for my spirit guides in my inner mental sanctuary, ready to receive any counsel they might have for me. After a little while the guide I will call M arrived, informing me that we had an important errand in the City of Lights.

I had first found that celestial city—and been warned away—many years earlier in a meditation. I still remember the awesome feeling of approaching it for the first time and experiencing a tremendous loving power. A kindly old man, who years later I discovered was one of my guides, met me at the gates of the city and warned me to stay away. I wasn't ready to be in a place, he said, where thoughts instantly manifested.

I beat a hasty mental retreat, appreciating anew how little control I actually had over my thoughts and what a disaster it would be if they all came to life. In the years that followed I had sometimes contemplated that city from a distance and on a few occasions ventured into one of its outer arcades. This morning, however, I was ushered in by my guide across a walkway made of glowing cubes of light. We proceeded directly to the Hall of Past Lives, where there was a large book with my name on it, containing the entire history of my soul from the moment it had been born in the One Light. I was also shown a computer screen where any psychological pattern could be entered to call up a past life relating to it.

The pattern of fear that I might unconsciously hurt or betray another person had improved somewhat over the previous year with the retrieval of the first two past-life memories, but it still came up on occasion, and I knew that there was more territory to be covered on the way to freedom. So I punched in "paranoid fear" on the cosmic computer, and up came the image of a beautiful young woman being walked down a dark corridor to a dungeon. M told me that to see any more of the lifetime now would be upsetting, but that the time was near for clearing out the karmic pattern that it represented.

While meditating on Yom Kippur, the Day of Atonement, I was brought back to the City of Lights, where I wrote my resolutions for the New Year in the book of my life. I strongly affirmed that this would be the year for transcending past negativity. Affirmations made consciously in the presence of God are powerful prayers.

The answer to my prayer came in the form of two friends whose love and care reached across space and time to help me forgive others as well as myself and gain freedom from past karma. My reason for telling this story is that it illustrates a great cosmic law: "Knock and it shall be opened." The door that opens for any person who says a heartfelt prayer is unique because we are all unique. I certainly don't espouse past-life therapy for everybody. In most cases the working through of problems in this life is sufficient to bring us to new levels of realization and the finishing of old business. But for me the recall of past lives was a major turning point.

AN ANCIENT TALE

The weekend of the fall equinox, one of the two passages of the yearly cycle when the hours of darkness are exactly equivalent to the hours of light, marked the fifth community healing circle that Myrin and I had hosted. Our dear friend, Tricia Stallman, was near the end of her gentle, beautiful life. She and her husband, Alvin, had requested that we hold the healing circle at their house since she was too weak to get out of bed. As was usual with Tricia, she was joyful, even in her waning strength. She was upstairs in her bed and about fifty of us were downstairs in the living room. When our songs began to reflect our sadness that Trish was completing her sojourn here, she banged on the ceiling and sent us a message to pick up the beat— she wasn't gone yet!

On the hour-long drive back to our house, Myrin and two of our friends were reflecting on Trish's joy, and on her healing. We all hoped that when our time to die came we would be as whole as she was—our business finished, our hearts at peace and our souls free of the regrets and resentments that keep us in bondage. The discussion about healing and breaking free from what Eastern philosophy calls the Wheel of Birth and Death continued when we got home. One of the women present was our friend Elena Burton, a physician and Jungian analyst. Myrin and I had known Elena for two years, and she was a frequent visitor, often using our house for short retreats. Oddly, although I knew that Elena did past-life regressions as part of her work, we had never spoken of it in any depth.

Elena told us that she reserved past-life regression work for certain circumstances in which the client had expended all other routes of investigation and had a clear and pressing issue to explore. A light went on in my head. I was just such a person, and the best therapist I could imagine, one who we knew and trusted implicitly, was staying in our own house. We scheduled a past-life regression for the following morning, which was the actual day of the equinox and also a full moon.

We chose a comfortable, sacred space for the session—the floor of the study, which is also my sanctuary. Its walls are lined with books. My trusty Macintosh stands ever-ready on the big white desk that looks out over a weeping cherry tree. To the right of the desk is a meditation chapel, a small triangular room that is actually a closet with the doors removed. In it is a simple shrine—a low table that holds a candle, a chalice and a few sacred objects. Pictures of family, friends, animals and saints peek from various corners, and a faint smell of incense suffuses the room.

Elena made a nest on the rose-plush carpet, covering a yoga mat with a blanket so that I could lie down comfortably for what turned out to be nearly a three-hour session. After a brief stop at the shrine to pray, Elena covered me with a pink-and-blue patchwork quilt. Her voice was soft, comforting and matter-of-fact. We were going to make a journey into the soul, a journey of healing and wisdom. As my breathing became slow and regular in response to her wise, quiet presence, she asked if there was any power animal whose help I wanted to enlist. Immediately I found myself on the back of a familiar animal friend (it is thought best to keep the identity of these animal helpers secret, so you can imagine this helping spirit anyway you wish), traveling through a dark, watery underworld.

After a time we came up into a desolate, windswept landscape. Lonely moors extended to a leaden sea that seemed to stretch endlessly to the horizon. Wind whistled through the stone windows of a small, abandoned castle whose foyer had been taken over by tall weeds. "Where are you?" Elena's voice queried from another world.

"The north coast of England," I replied, feeling chilly and oddly discomforted. I could "see" with my inner eyes that a skeleton was buried in the hard-packed dirt floor in the basement of the castle. Elena asked me if I wanted to stay and explore this castle or move on to another time. I was undecided, so she instructed me to ask the soul of the person whose skeleton was buried there. As is typical in the imaginal realm, there was no hunting around for the soul. My intent to find it brought me together instantly with a man I recognized as my father from that lifetime.

Seeing this dear man face to face drew me into a vivid experience of a lifetime in thirteenth-century England at the time when the distant horror of the Crusades was abating, only to coalesce in the guise of local persecution. In that lifetime I was the daughter, and youngest of three children, of a petty monarch whose seaside kingdom was large but agriculturally poor. Born clairvoyant, from earliest childhood I was prone to terrifying visions in which my middle brother, George, plotted to kill my father and older brother, William, who would otherwise inherit the lands.

My father put the visions aside as hysterical, cautioning me to tell no one. Although he never quite believed me, he did feel that I could be in danger if news that I was prescient reached the Church authorities, who might persecute me as a witch. My mother was simply too fragile and easily upset to listen. Depressed by the cold, dreary coast of England and yearning for her childhood home in the sunny climes of southern France, she spent much of her days lost in fantasies of her youth. I was left alone with my fears and might have gone mad were it not for Martha, my kind nursemaid.

At seventeen, which was late in those times, I was married to an Italian man with the unlikely name of Morgan. He had made a name for himself in the Crusades and had come to England at the bidding of Church authorities. He was the first person in my life who took my clairvoyance seriously. In his country, he confided, all decisions in places of power were reached after consultation with seers. He was happy to have my counsel. As for the matter of my father and George, he told me not to worry. He would protect my father and my older brother. I felt some peace at last.

But my happiness was short-lived. I soon became pregnant with our first child, little Anna. As the pregnancy progressed, my psychic sight dimmed and was lost completely at her birth. Morgan was infuriated both by the birth of a girl—he had wanted a male heir—and by the loss of my powers. We became more and more estranged. A little more than a year after Anna's birth I had a second child, Michael. Although I had hoped that Morgan's happiness in having a son would mend our relationship, he grew even more distant.

I lived happily enough in my own world, though. Martha, my old nursemaid, had accompanied me when I married Morgan and now helped with Anna and Michael, who were beautiful, bright children. I was sitting in our rooms one day with the three of them when my clairvoyance returned and I had a horrible vision, one that I relived with stunning emotional intensity.

As I began to sob and moan, Elena gently encouraged me to cry out my grief and tell her what was happening. In the vision I was one with my father. It was as if my soul was in his body and I was experiencing life from his perspective. My husband, Morgan, had just run him through with a lance, and at the same moment my dear father witnessed his son George killing his other son, William. There are no words that can convey the anguish of that hideous betrayal. The terror of the scene was compounded for me in my father's dying thoughts. Since my husband was his killer, he believed that not only George but also I had betrayed him.

After moving forward in time from that prodigious trauma I relived the sad details of the several months that passed after the slaughter of my father and brother. Elena then brought me forward in time to the last week of my life in that incarnation. My treacherous brother and husband had turned me over to the Church as a witch. Found guilty, I was condemned to death by starvation and dehydration. As I was led down a long hall to a dungeon where other women were being held, I recognized the same scene that had been revealed in meditation in the Hall of Past Lives, before M had counseled me against seeing more of that lifetime.

The women in that dungeon heard my story with interest and compassion, comforting the young woman who had tried for a lifetime to protect her father and brother, only to be thought of as the betrayer. Later that afternoon, one of the women died. It was a luminous death; light and transcendent peace filled the room. From another dimension, she promised to meet me at the moment of my own death and give me safe passage to the Other Side. Elena then brought me forward to the moment of my death in that lifetime. There, in the presence of the Light, I was reconciled with my father.

I lay exhausted after reliving this story, tended to by dear Elena, whose loving presence was strongly reminiscent of the circle of women in that dungeon. Elena and I reviewed the regression from the perspective of betrayal. In that lifetime I was the betrayed, yet my greatest pain was that my father had thought me the betrayer. Elena reminded me again of the soul's need to live both roles and then transcend them through forgiveness.

The inability to forgive myself for incidents that elicited the shadow of betrayal in this life were inexorably linked to residual anger I still held against George and Morgan from a lifetime 800 years ago. How's that for holding a grudge? The Sermon on the Mount is succinct in its teaching on freedom. To be forgiven we must forgive. Bound by an unforgiveness that was entirely unconscious until the regression awakened my memories, I was still reenacting the drama of betrayer and betrayed in one of its endless permutations. That knowledge allowed me to reach back through time and forgive those ancient actors in the theater of souls, thus finding a new level of kindness toward myself.

Old soul memories not only give us the chance to finish old business; they also provide an opportunity to appreciate the love and beauty that exist even in difficult times. The memory of this core lifetime reawakened a deep gratitude for the circle of women who had given one another safe passage in times of old. I have the same deep gratitude for the circle of women who I am privileged to share this life with now, some of whom you've already met in the preceding pages and one of whom you will meet next as she steps across the dream world to weave another thread into the tapestry of wholeness.

THE CIRCLE OF WOMEN

About a week after Elena took me through that past-life regression, some practical pointers for chasing away the shadows of fear were added by another close friend and colleague, Robin Casarjian. Robin is a therapist and the author of a wonderful book, *Forgiveness: A Bold Choice for a Peaceful Heart.* In addition to seeing clients and conducting workshops, she is also the founder and director of the Lionheart Foundation, which sponsors workshops on forgiveness in prisons. Through the years Robin has been a steadfast and loving support and a teacher of forgiveness, trust and balance.

Robin, Elena and I were conducting a weekend workshop called "Deep Healing: Mending the Wound of Unworthiness" at a conference center in western Massachusetts. Robin and I drove there together, managing to get lost while deep in conversation. We arrived exhausted on Friday evening, just in time to meet Elena and have dinner, and for me to conduct the evening session. It was midnight before we got to bed in adjoining rooms.

I had a dream that night that I entitled "Karma Is Ending." It begins as a nightmare in which I am being pursued by an energy that has been incompletely destroyed and keeps coming back in the form of little creatures like the brooms from "The Sorcerer's Apprentice." The more I try to destroy them, the more they reproduce themselves! All the creatures finally disappear, but I am on my guard, awaiting their return. I am in a leader role with a group of people who are sharing in this adventure and seem to be learning a lot from it. We are safe for the moment but expect the energy to manifest next as an attack from a swooping flock of seagulls. Instead, we see it marching down the street as a line of mechanical, wire-mesh mice. They aren't scary at all.

It doesn't take a dream expert to see how "Karma Is Ending" related to the working out of an old energy pattern that had been incompletely resolved and kept coming back as fearsome attacks. When the energy was faced at last, the fear lost its power and become a teacher, returning as a humorous shadow of its former self.

Robin also had a dream that night. As we walked up the long road from our lodgings to the hall where breakfast was served, she told us that the dream didn't seem to be about her issues at all. Instead, it seemed to be about mine. In the dream, Robin, who is a very circumspect person, shares details about one of her client's problems with a therapist from whom she is getting peer supervision. The other therapist unthinkingly tells these details to someone else and word gets back to Robin's client, who is justifiably incensed. Robin's dream reaction reflects her waking-life attitudes of responsibility and trust. A very unfortunate episode has occurred in which her client was inadvertently hurt. She wishes that it hadn't happened, but it did. So she tells herself, "This is what has happened, and whatever happens, I can handle it."

This simple dream presented the type of incident that would previously have created terrible fear and anguish for me. At the moment when Robin shared it, there was a kind of felt-shift. The truth espoused by the medieval poet Wolfram Von Eschenbach, in the first line of his poem about the Holy Grail, registered at a new level of awareness: "Every act has both good and evil results. The best we can do is to intend the good." I needed to let go of worrying about what the results of every action might be and just intend the good. If unfortunate results occurred, well, "This is what has happened, and whatever happens I can handle it."

And so it is. Robin's affirmation became a practical tool that I use whenever I am tempted to give life to old patterns of fear that come up when I fantasize that some act of mine might have untoward results. I know that we cannot control the universe. Despite our best efforts, difficult circumstances will still arise. We are always learning, always growing, always hitting against the walls of our self-made cages as the urge to freedom swells within our breasts. And if we remember that the power of love supports us and that seen and unseen helpers will emerge to help us whenever we pray for assistance, we will find the courage to free ourselves from the bonds of the past.

CHAPTER EIGHT

Night Vision— Courage, Hope and Optimism

There are no guarantees. From the viewpoint of fear none are strong enough. From the viewpoint of love none are necessary.

Emmanuel

Do you remember the story of the Cowardly Lion from *The Wizard of Oz?* Led by the intrepid Dorothy, he and the Straw Man and the Tin Man sought the power of Oz to give them courage, brains and a heart respectively. The wizard turned out to be a sham—a humbug, he called himself—in that he had no magic power to create change from without. He was a true teacher, though, in his ability to bring forth change from within.

The wizened old man who had masqueraded as the Great Oz said to the Cowardly Lion, "You have plenty of courage, I am sure. *All you need is confidence in yourself* [italics added]. There is no living thing that is not afraid when it faces danger. True courage is in facing danger when you are afraid, and that kind of courage you have in plenty."

The lion, however, did not believe that courage was within, so the wizard had to resort to the placebo effect to cure him. Setting a bowl of green liquid in front of the shamefaced beast, Oz commanded the lion to drink it. "What is it?" asked the lion.

"Well," answered Oz, "if it were inside of you it would be courage. You know, of course, that courage is always inside one; so that this really cannot be called courage until you have swallowed it. Therefore I advise you to drink it as soon as possible." The lion, tricked into remembering what was already within, went forth and took up his rightful position as courageous king of the forest.

STAGE 1: WILLFUL COURAGE

The kind of courage that the Wizard of Oz taught the lion is what I call Stage 1, or willful courage. I first discovered it personally in recovering from obsessive-compulsive disorder as a ten-year-old. I rediscovered it half a lifetime later when I was a twenty-year-old college junior and my snake nightmare from a decade earlier began to recur.

Fearful that I might slide back into the rituals, I reluctantly sought help. The Paoli local train hummed reassuringly on the rails as it ate up the seventeen miles between the suburb of Bryn Mawr, where I went to college, and the downtown Philadelphia office of the psychiatrist I had chosen as my ally. It took two sessions for me to tell him the story of my twenty years. At the third session, I wanted to get right into the recurrent nightmare in which my mother dispatched me into the dangerous waters where the giant serpent erupted from the deep. The psychiatrist was more of a pragmatist than I was. I was after the symbolism, the mystery, a hidden key to the meaning of my fears. He was after my mother. The session ended with his brandishing the phone in the air, challenging me to confront her.

"Whadaya say I call her?" He held my eyes with his. "Maybe I can get her on the phone right now. You can tell her exactly what's wrong with your relationship—how you really feel, how you wish things could be between you?" I remember the cold fingers of fear clutching at my belly. I was ready to tackle a symbolic serpent, but the thought of an honest conversation with a real mother was absolutely out of the question.

I bolted from his office and never returned. My dream, my free-floating anxiety and I were on our own again. This was nothing new. I was used to living with fear, so I gave myself a pep talk similar to the one I had used when I was ten. "You have to pull yourself together now. You have to get back to living your life. All those other women (my college classmates) are doing well. You are just as good as they are. Now buck up and get on with things before you really mess everything up."

I acted from the only courage I knew—the application of a strong will that allowed me to function *in spite* of fear. Although this strategy allowed me to keep going, it kept me stuck where I was and prevented the healing of my relationship with my mother, a fact that I sincerely regret. Like many privileged women of her era, she had been raised to believe that success for a woman lay in marrying a wealthy man. Doing right for her daughter meant teaching me perfect manners, making sure I took the right lessons (piano, ballet, singing, elocution, ballroom dancing), criticizing and correcting any and all defects in my body or behavior to improve my chances of attracting Prince Charming, and systematically discouraging any intellectual curiosity that might make me seem threatening to a man. This she did with an iron hand.

In retrospect I understand that she was trying to ensure a good life for me in the best way she knew. But at twenty I felt controlled, criticized, frustrated, unacknowledged, angry and stifled. I wanted to be a scientist and to marry my high school sweetheart, whom she didn't approve of. The rift between us seemed unbridgeable. My life had to be lived on her terms or else I was a failure in her eyes.

In spite of her rigidity, she was in many ways an exceptional woman—loyal, strong and possessed of a world-class sense of humor. She was close to death before we healed our relationship when I was in my early forties. I miss the years of closeness that we might have shared if I hadn't bolted from that psychiatrist's office and turned down his offer to teach me about Stage 2 courage—the willingness to be honest, to face old pain, to heal the past and to become myself.

STAGE 2: PSYCHOLOGICAL COURAGE

As infants we are completely helpless. Bonded with our primary caretaker, often the mother, we have no separate sense of self. Mommy and I are one. In the best of situations, mother mirrors baby. If baby coos, mother coos. If baby cries with hunger, mother responds with milk. If baby is tired and needs to sleep, mother leaves baby to rest. If baby is fascinated with her toes, mother takes delight in that fascination without interrupting it. But if Mommy is out of synchrony with our rhythm—absent when we need her or intrusive when we need space—then we feel out of joint with life. A gap or crevice opens between us and our most important other, and this hole in the soul accompanies us throughout life like an aching emptiness that nothing can fill.

The hole in the soul that forms during infancy often widens in early childhood. My own overprotective mother frequently intruded on my need for space and tried to mold me in her own image. I was lovable when and if I met her conditions. Good mothering, in her eyes, meant badgering me into conforming rather than facilitating the development of my own uniqueness. As I discuss in *Guilt Is the Teacher, Love Is the Lesson,* this kind of conditional love, with its implied threat of abandonment if we don't measure up, is terrifying to a small child. It feels like a death threat.

To insulate ourselves from that threat, we develop a cast of false selves, or masks, that get us attention. The perfectionist, the victim, the joker, the rescuer, the saint, the people pleaser, the troublemaker—these are some common false selves that might have assured approval and attention or kept us relatively safe as children. If, as adults, we come to believe that these masks are who we really are, we end up feeling anxious and empty of ourselves. The hole in the soul gapes wider, and we may try to fill it with food, alcohol, drugs, needy relationships, workaholism, sex or material goods.

Empty was a good description of how I felt at twenty. I didn't know who I was. A perfectionistic overachiever on the outside, I was filled with shame and self-doubt on the inside. My conclusion was that my true identity was that of a loser and a fraud. If people really knew who I was, I reasoned, they would hate me. No wonder I felt anxious!

Recognizing and dismantling our masks is a necessary part of developing psychological courage and discovering our true identity. In *Guilt Is the Teacher, Love Is the Lesson*, I suggest working with your inner child—the younger self or selves who still persist within yearning for respect, comfort, understanding and the chance to grow into a wise, loving adult. "Sam," for example, was in his forties when I first saw him in therapy for asthma and chronic bronchitis. When I asked him if he had any memories of what was happening in his life when the asthma began, he nodded sadly. His early life had been idyllic until, at age eight, his whole world had suddenly collapsed. His father was killed in an industrial accident when a crane malfunctioned. His mother, left with Sam and three younger children, became depressed. The children were separated and shipped to the homes of different relatives for three years while the mother recovered.

Sam's response was typical of a child—he blamed himself. He thought that his mother's breakdown was his fault because he had not helped her enough. He was determined thereafter to be a good boy in every way, to redeem himself for his fantasized failure. Sam couldn't stand to get dirty; it made more wash for his aunt, to whose house he had moved after his mother's breakdown. He helped constantly around the house, often shunning play in favor of helping with the chores or studying. Sam forgot how to feel joy, repressing his spontaneity and locking it deep inside. After all, he had reasoned in his child mind, if he had been more serious and helpful his mother would never have gotten ill. If he had done his new job as "man of the house" better after his father died, the family could have stayed together. The tensions that Sam felt at that time manifested themselves as asthma.

As an adult, Sam's asthma often worsened when people were angry with him or when he even suspected that he might have disappointed them. At these times the unearned, unhealthy guilt he was still carrying from his childhood erupted as strong anxiety—leftover feelings from the time when his family broke apart. Sam tried to keep the guilt and fear at bay by going out of his way to be helpful, apologetic, nice and cooperative. Bending over backward to help others, he was in the habit of ignoring himself. Sam's every move was dictated by the fear of disappointing someone.

The grief and shame Sam had suffered as a child were still locked into his body and behaviors. They had never been healed, a four-fold process consisting of mourning for the childhood loss, experiencing the anger that naturally accompanies loss, understanding the situation from an adult perspective and forgiving oneself and the others who were involved. This process of deep healing opens the heart and creates compassion for self and others.

As Sam began to grieve, he encountered parts of himself that he had lost touch with. Parts of his wholeness, such as joy and anger, had been disowned in his childhood and consigned to his shadow, to Robert Bly's "long bag" that we carry with us through life until we find the courage to open it up and empty it out. In *A Little Book on the Human Shadow*, Bly comments that "we spend our life until we're twenty deciding what parts of ourself to put into the bag, and we spend the rest of our lives trying to get them out again."

The process of dismantling the mask and pulling our wholeness back out of the bag is psychological courage in action. Facing and transforming old pain in this mode of gradual self-discovery can sometimes promote physical healing as well. In Sam's case, for example, his asthma was clearly related to childhood trauma and the consequent splitting of his personality into mask and shadow. In addition to helping Sam learn bodily self-regulation techniques, including meditation, belly breathing and the use of creative imagination to dilate his bronchial passages, I set him to work healing his inner eight-year-old.

In the process of healing, both Sam's asthma and his fear dissipated significantly. When I saw him at follow-up about six months after we had first met, his whole demeanor had changed. He was more relaxed and joyful. The tension was gone from his face and he looked ten years younger. As it was with Sam, a decision to face our pain, whether physical or emotional, is the first step in developing psychological courage—the will to be aware, to reclaim our lost selves and to mend the hole in our soul.

In that fascinating, challenging process of soul mending and self-discovery, it is inevitable that we will think about the age-old questions "Who am I?" and "What is the meaning of life?" from the new perspective that we have gained. It is in this broadening of perspective that spiritual courage is found. This third stage of courage is revealed naturally and gradually when the filters through which we had previously seen life fall from our eyes and we begin to catch glimpses of the infinite love from which the entire drama is spun.

STAGE 3: SPIRITUAL COURAGE

The mystic poet William Blake said, "If the doors of perception were cleansed, man would see everything as it is, infinite." Psychological courage entails just such a cleansing of the doors of perception, allowing us to see things as they really are rather than through the distorted lens of the past. The more we are cleansed of expectations, the more we see what is and the more we can respond to it creatively.

In those moments when we are fully present to life—the moments of grace—we experience love, gratitude, awe, joy, security and compassion. There is no fear. We know this when we are in the midst of a rapture, transported by the stark beauty of a mountain path or lost in the eyes of our beloved. We know this when we abandon our little selves and find our greater Selves in song or dance. We know this when an amazing serendipity delights us and we are reminded again that coincidence, as the old saying goes, is just God's way of remaining anonymous. Unfortunately, we tend to forget it the rest of the time. Spiritual courage grows through our willingness to keep on remembering, to keep on searching for the sacred behind all the seemingly mundane and even terrible facets of life.

Spiritual courage is more than faith that the universe is friendly and that, despite all earthly appearance to the contrary, we are ultimately safe. It is the *inner knowing* that this is so. That knowing is the composite of all our experiences, dreams, serendipities and practices of remembering—such as meditations and prayers as well as the "tingles of recognition" and "aha's" we feel when someone else's story awakens our remembering and becomes part of our soul-knowledge.

My own courage was given a considerable boost as a result of a remarkable series of events that surrounded the death of my mother in March 1988. Although her death from emphysema and congestive heart failure was slow and must surely have been quite uncomfortable as her heart and lungs failed and her body swelled like a water balloon, she rarely complained. Not a woman to show her emotions in life, she didn't reveal them at death's door either. In her final hours, Mom's manner of finishing old business was simple and direct. She turned her face up at me as we rode together in an elevator on the way back from one final test, saying, "I've made a lot of mistakes in my life. Will you forgive me, Joanie?"

I squeezed her hand and replied simply and in kind, "I forgive you, Mom. I've made a lot of mistakes, too. Will you forgive me?" She nodded, and we rode in silence to her room. My brother was there with his children. My husband and two sons were there. Other relatives, friends and the two loyal women who had cared for my mother during her long illness were there as well, all gathered to say their last good-byes.

The sun was setting already, casting long shadows on a cold Saint Patrick's Day evening that held the barest hint of the coming spring. The hospital windows overlooked the Boston skyline, and the lights of the city began to awaken in the violet twilight. It was the last time we would experience a sunset together. We held hands, she lying still and heavy on the white sheets, supported by pillows since she was too weak to keep herself from falling to the side. This formidable woman looked so vulnerable and yet so at peace.

"Mom," I began, looking into remarkably sweet and innocent eyes, eyes that used to sparkle with mischief and would often flash with anger. "Mom, I want to exchange gifts with you. I want to exchange a special quality, a soul quality that we admire in one another." I hesitated for a moment, wondering if this sensible, concrete woman would think I was crazy. She clearly did not. Moved by her vulnerability and by a feeling of mutual trust, I continued, "I have always admired your courage. I ask it as a gift from you."

She smiled at me and pressed my hand with her waning strength. "I give you courage," she said. "And I ask you for compassion."

There was so much love in that moment. She saw me as compassionate. (As I typed this last sentence, by the way, my unconscious reversed the letters in "saw." I typed she "was" me as compassionate. That slip, perhaps, captures the essence of our bonding better than words do.) I felt seen, acknowledged, valued. I never thought of her as admiring compassion, nor did I expect she would have seen it in me since I had often been more angry than compassionate to her in the forty-three years of our relationship. Perhaps she was also surprised that I saw her as courageous, but I did. She personified that first kind of courage—indomitable will, the ability to keep on trucking no matter what.

Mom drifted in and out of consciousness for the rest of the evening. She sometimes spoke of seeing the Light, returning to consciousness fully in character, cracking a few last jokes before she slipped into a final morphine-assisted sleep. Our son Justin, my brother, Alan, and I stayed with her that long night as she labored to give birth to her soul. We sang to her, held her, prayed for her, sat with her and alternately roamed the hospital corridors.

At one point I sat meditating in her room and was suddenly overcome by a vivid vision that pulled me out of normal, waking consciousness into another realm. It was a luminous kind of experience during which every cell in my body felt wonderfully alive, and I knew that I was witnessing a deeper reality than is usually perceptible.

In the vision I was a pregnant mother, laboring to give birth to a baby. Remarkably, I was simultaneously the baby in the process of being born. Although the birth superficially involved pain and fear, it was deeply joyful, peaceful and transcendent. As the mother I felt the holiness of being a gateway into life. As the baby I was in wondrous awe of the bright, mysterious and awesome Light I saw at the end of the long, dark tunnel of birth. From the perspective of being both mother and child, I felt totally at one with my mother. Our life together—in all its joys, sorrows, angers and anguishes— made perfect sense. I was aware of her consciousness moving down the dark tunnel and leaving this world, already rejoicing in the splendor of her return to the Light. She had birthed me into this world, and I felt as though I had birthed her out of it.

I opened my eyes to a room that seemed to be suffused with the Light and alive with an indescribable, peaceful power. My twenty-year-old son, Justin, was also in the room. He turned to me and said in awed tones, "I feel like Grandma is holding open the door to eternity to give us a glimpse. Can you feel it?"

Although Mother's body continued to breathe for a few more hours until an oxygen tube was removed, it felt as if her soul had been born back to the Other Side in the silence of the night. The memory of our last exchange and of the extraordinary vision stayed with me, creating a new frame of reference through which our sometimes difficult relationship appeared whole and perfect. I no longer thought in terms of forgiveness—her forgiving me or me forgiving her. The deep acceptance and identification I felt with her during those last few hours left me with an expanded view of our life together. That fuller viewpoint, an expanded vision in which even pain and disappointment make perfect sense as part of the fabric of divine love, is really at the heart of Stage 3, or spiritual courage. When I asked her for the gift of courage that night, I had no idea what a revelation would follow.

I dreamed of Mom several times in the weeks following her passing. Although they were varied—funny, mysterious, delightful, painful, symbolic and healing—each dream was like a jewel. In one of the dreams she reminded me that she was often a bitch and that I'd better not start idealizing her! In another dream, I collected her gift of courage which allowed me to face both the pain of this life and of the past lives I described in the previous chapters. The experience of courage that was given to me in the dream imprinted a new story on my soul and sent me forth into waking life with a changed perspective.

In the dream I am in the mountains, passing through on my way to give a workshop. Noticing a hidden door in the side of the mountain, I enter a room full of people. I am told it is a café but soon discover that I am in a school for spies. Several old women are there. They tell me how the school has pushed them to their very limits of endurance—sometimes beyond their limits. These women glow with wisdom, confidence, strength, compassion and power. I feel a fierce willingness and desire to submit myself to the same tests they have endured. It dawns on me that I have just been accepted into a school for courage.

The time comes for the final exam. As the class passes through a room, I am drawn to a group of children playing. When I look up, I realize that the class has gone on without me. I have to find my way to the final test myself. I know only to look for a hole in the ground.

Outside once again I come upon a hollow tree trunk. Inside looms a giant, dark, watery chasm. Surprising myself, I jump immediately inside, abandoning myself completely to the watery darkness. Unexpectedly I land on a raft and travel at breakneck speed through a dark underground tunnel of water. I feel complete confidence and know at some deep level that my relation to fear and to the unknown have changed. Emerging into a landscape of stunning brightness and beauty I awaken feeling joyful and very clear.

I recorded the dream in my journal and then got up to make coffee. There by the coffee pot was a round sticker, the kind that adheres when you peel the back off. It was, and is, about three inches in diameter, red with swirly white lettering that, at first glance, seems to spell "Coca-Cola." It doesn't. It actually spells "courage." The red badge of courage awaited me with the morning coffee. I asked my sons and husband where it had come from. No one knew. It is currently mounted in my office over my word processor. I can see it as I write. I often look at it or remember it in those moments when fear has narrowed my vision and I have lost a higher perspective.

COURAGE AND LUCIDITY

As I reflected on my dream about courage I often wondered about the meaning of being accepted into a school for spies, literally *a school for the clear seeing of what is really happening*. The answer came to me as an "aha" while I read a book by psychotherapist Kenneth Kelzer called *The Sun and the Shadow: My Experiment with Lucid Dreaming*. A lucid dream is a dream in which you become aware that you are dreaming without waking up. Most people have occasionally had such dreams, and with practice (as discussed by Kelzer and others) the majority of people can enter the lucid dream state with some regularity. Although I have only become lucid a handful of times, I can remember each of the dreams in detail. At the moment when you suddenly realize, "Aha, ducks don't have red fur, I must be dreaming," it feels like a sudden awakening into a whole new level of consciousness.

The lucid state feels "realer than real." Sense perceptions are heightened, and everything seems much more vivid than it does either in waking life or in the ordinary dream state, almost as if it were being lighted from within. One's body also feels radically alive. Awareness on all levels is pleasurably heightened, and it seems as though a veil that conceals the beauty and magic of life has been drawn aside to reveal things in their original splendor. For me, a lucid dream is a special treat, a temporary ticket back home to a state of greater consciousness and freedom.

In his book, Kelzer comments that when you become lucid in a dream you automatically move beyond fear. I was intrigued by his discussion, because it dovetailed with my own experience. As I thought back over my lucid dreams, I could appreciate that the courage I had felt in some of them was not based on a state of will where I actively opposed the bad things that were happening and hoped for the best. *Instead, courage flowed from an altered state of perception—a true clarity—in which I knew at some level that the fearful situation was, in fact, an exciting opportunity to expand my awareness and wisdom. Furthermore, I knew that I was completely and absolutely safe.*

The transcendent, spiritual courage that emerges during the lucid dream state has at least three roots that I can recognize. First, in this special altered state of consciousness you *know* that you are dreaming. It is obvious that scary events are only parts of a transient drama. Second, while lucid you become strongly aware of a wellspring of tremendous inner power. (Once, while being pursued by a frightening dream figure, I suddenly realized I was dreaming and became lucid. My whole dreambody began to tingle and I felt superalive, superpowerful. I decided to stop running and confront my pursuer, who was particularly dangerous because she had supernatural powers. I felt invincible and was immediately able to end the threat creatively.) Third, lucidity carries with it a strong conviction that the overcoming of fear by some act of creativity represents true soul growth.

The Tibetans, in their ancient spiritual literature, discuss the "yoga of the dream state," which was their term for cultivating lucidity in dreams. Since life itself is viewed as a kind of dream, the cultivation of lucidity was desired to allow people to awaken within the dream of life and thereby act with fearlessness and compassion. In addition,

The Tibetan Book of the Dead discusses the Bardo states, realms that the soul visits after it leaves the body and encounters the Clear Light of loving consciousness. According to this philosophy, if one can remain lucid upon leaving the body at death, then the soul can travel through the Bardo states and discern their illusory nature, always orienting toward the real Light. In this way, the soul's karmic chains are broken and there is no need for rebirth.

In *The Sun and the Shadow*, Kelzer summarizes as follows the experience of finding courage during a potentially frightening dream in which he became lucid:

> There is a kind of magic in many lucid dreams. This one had the potential to became a nightmare, but in the moment that I became lucid I experienced total inner transformation. All my fear vanished in an instant, and inside of myself I felt full of courage. Complete clarity of vision, in this dream, yielded instant transformation. This became one of the most important principles that I learned from this particular lucid dream. To see *fully* is to have courage. To see *fully* is to have no fear (p. 5).

One of major oddities of existence is that we can see more clearly in the lucid dream state than we generally do in waking life. Our ordinary waking perceptions are clouded by past experience and the brainwashing of society that teaches us to live by avoiding fear rather than by realizing love. Dark nights of the soul challenge us to wake up from our dreams of limitation and claim the freedom that is our destiny. As the Apostle Paul wrote of that awakening, "We see now but through a glass darkly, but then we shall see face to face."

TO SEE CLEARLY: FACE TO FACE WITH THE LIGHT

When is the "then" Paul talks about when we will see face to face? We have glimpses of clear vision throughout our life, not just in the "clear light" that accompanies the experience of death, according to both ancient philosophies and those 5 percent of Americans who have had near-death experiences. People report moments of clear vision—of entering a state of mind that seems "realer than real"—in predeath visions that precede actual physical death, in transcendent visions that are not associated with death, in lucid dreams, in meditation, in flashes of intuition and in the common "holy moments" or epiphanies that all of us experience from time to time.

When these moments of clear vision last long enough, we understand that we have just glimpsed beyond the veil that separates the apparent world we live in from a richer, fuller world that literally appears luminous or light-filled. The common expression "to see the light" means to reach a deeper level of understanding. When we see the Light there is no more fear, because we have seen beyond it into the radiance that is love itself. In the presence of love, things make sense. We become present to wisdom.

Pediatrician Melvin Morse is one of the country's foremost researchers in the field of near-death experiences. He became interested in them after several children he had resuscitated began to share the experiences of the ineffable Light they had experienced on the Other Side. In his beautiful book *Closer to the Light: Learning from the Near-death Experiences of Children,* Dr. Morse discusses the difficulty that most children (and adults as well) have in describing the Light, since terms like "all-knowing," "all-forgiving" and "all-loving" cannot begin to capture the splendor of the actual experience.

One of the cases Dr. Morse describes involved a child called Terry who entered a coma and nearly died from accidentally eating several painkillers. As an adult she described her childhood experience of leaving her body while in the coma and traveling down a water-filled tunnel. Although the tunnel was dark, she was unafraid. The tunnel branched and she passed under an arch, emerging suddenly into a Light she described as "so beautiful that it couldn't be called a light. It represented love and peace and happiness and complete and utter joy." When she emerged from the experience, she reported seeing "pieces of the light everywhere. I could see how everything in the world fits together."

Dr. Morse reports that children who have had near-death experiences are remarkably mature, wise and compassionate toward others.

Upon reaching adolescence they almost never use drugs or alcohol, understanding at some level that these substances dim the Light rather than leading closer to it. In discussing the Light, Morse cites examples in which children have seen the Light without having had a near-death experience. He quotes Oxford scholar Edward Robinson, who describes a spiritual experience he had while walking on the beach with his mother as a four-year-old, in which flowers seemed to "shine with a brilliant fire." Robinson knew that this fire was the "living tissue of life." The feeling he had in that moment was of knowing his own special place in the order of things and feeling a certainty of "ultimate good."

Could we all have Robinson's experience of perceiving our own special place in the order of things, coupled with the realization that the tissue of life is love itself and the certainty of ultimate good, then we would have no fear. We would have the kind of spiritual courage and optimism that comes from a direct perception of what is.

I do believe that there are ways to learn the kind of spiritual courage that comes by grace to a few of us in visions, dreams and near-death experiences, as I'll discuss in Part Three. Of course, we don't have much need of courage until we face fear, and perhaps that is the best reason of all for our fear—it motivates us to find true courage through a heartfelt search for the sacred. But until we develop the courage and optimism that comes from seeing things clearly, we can cultivate the hope that our pain and fear is truly an initiation into Light.

HOPE AND SURRENDER

Hope is a term that is usually applied to the future. We hope that our health will stay good or, if we are ill, that it will improve. We hope that our children will do well, that there will be peace on earth, that we will have enough money to pay the bills. This kind of hope is directive, willful. As in Stage 1 courage born of will, we are "happy" only if we get what we wish for, if our will is done. Like spiritual courage, spiritual hope is most likely to emerge when we let go of will and open ourselves to trust. Brother David Steindl-Rast, a

Benedictine monk who is part of the contemplative movement to unite Eastern and Western spirituality, speaks of hope in his book *Gratefulness, The Heart of Prayer*.

> Some people imagine that hope is the highest degree of optimism, a kind of super-optimism. I get the image of someone climbing higher and higher to the most fanciful pinnacle of optimism, there to wave the little flag of hope. A far more accurate picture would be that hope happens when the bottom drops out of our pessimism. We have nowhere to fall but into the ultimate reality of God's motherly caring. That is why St. Paul tells us that "tribulation leads to patience; and patience to experience; and experience to hope" (p. 136).

Steindl-Rast points out that the ordeals we suffer purge us of unfounded optimism. When the "bottom drops out of our pessimism" we are forced to let go of the idea that we are "doers" who can conquer life by the application of our individual will. The first step of any twelve-step program addresses just this issue of the bottom dropping out. In the case of alcoholism, the step reads, "We realized that we were powerless over alcohol and that our lives had become unmanageable." We might apply this attitude of surrender to any area of life in which we have struggled fruitlessly to change.

At first glance, hope and surrender may seem to be strange bedfellows. But when, as Steindl-Rast says, we "fall into the ultimate reality of God's motherly caring," we find that we have landed in the lap of hope itself. Hope, he asserts, is a patient waiting for God, a stillness that allows us to hear the inner voice of guidance. In *Gratefulness, The Heart of Prayer*, he says,

> As long as we wait for an improvement of the situation our desires will make a great deal of noise. And if we wait for a deterioration of the situation, our fears will be noisy. The stillness that waits for the Lord's coming in any situation— that is the stillness of biblical hope. Not only is that stillness compatible with strenuous effort to change the situation,

if that is our God-given task. *It is only in that stillness that we shall clearly hear what our task is.* . . . The stillness of hope is the expression of a perfect focussing of energy on the task at hand. The stillness of hope is, therefore, the stillness of integrity. Hope integrates. It makes whole (italics added; pp. 138–139).

The Buddhists have a similar approach to finding hope in times of adversity and behaving in what they would call "right action." Rather than specifying to the universe what the situation means and what is required for it to be fixed, the Buddhist approach is one of openness, an attitude of "don't know." "Don't know" allows for stillness, and stillness for wisdom. From this perspective, hope is not at all a future wish, but a *depth of understanding* that can transform past and future as well as lead to conscious action that helps to shape future events.

Seen in this manner, hope is really a matter of perspective. Perspective comes from the Latin root *perspicere,* meaning "to look through." It has to do with the courage that comes from seeing clearly. In discouragement, the opposite pertains. Our vision is clouded, and we feel hopeless and lost. In his book *Healing Visualizations,* psychiatrist Gerald Epstein tells of meeting a famous Israeli psychotherapist, Colette Aboulker-Muscat, who has an international reputation for her ability to help heal people both physically and emotionally through the creative engagement of their imagination. Disenchanted with the practice of Freudian psychoanalysis, which often brings about change slowly, if at all, he sought out Madame Aboulker-Muscat to see how she used imagery to create new perspectives that in turn led to changed patterns of belief, behavior and bodily function.

Madame Aboulker-Muscat told Epstein that Freud had likened psychoanalysis to a train. Looking out at the passing landscape, patients would describe what they saw to the analyst sitting in the next seat. Turning to Epstein, she suddenly demanded of him, "In what direction does a train go?" He moved his arm horizontally to indicate the usual axis of a train ride. Aboulker-Muscat suddenly changed Epstein's perspective by moving her hand upward, "Well, what if the direction were changed to this axis?" Epstein writes,

I cannot detail what went through my mind at that moment. I am not sure that I knew then. What I did know, and still know as the truth of that moment, is that I felt an overwhelming sense of self-recognition, what is called an "aha" experience. It was an epiphany. The vertical movement [of Aboulker-Muscat's arm] seemed to lift me from the horizontal hold of the given, the ordinary patterns of everyday cause and effect. I leapt into freedom, and I saw that the task of therapy—the task of being human—was to help realize freedom, to go beyond the given, to the newness that we all are capable of, and to our capacity to renew and re-create (p. 126).

Hope is the ability Epstein speaks of to renew and recreate. It comes when we lift ourselves out of the familiar axis and see life from a higher perspective. Harris Dientsfrey, who quoted this story about Epstein in his fine book *Where the Mind Meets the Body,* comments, "From the train that moves horizontally—Freud's train—one can see only the details of the present rushing by to become the past. From the train that moves vertically off the earth into the sky— Aboulker-Muscat's train—one sees events that on the earth are variously past, present and future, but in the air are all present, a single vision."

The lens of hope through which past, present and future can assume new meanings is always awaiting the triumphant birth of newness. When our youngest son, Andrei, was sixteen, he was at the pinnacle (or the nadir, depending on your perspective) of his adolescence. Moody and confused, he was often less than pleasant to be around. Nonetheless, with a mother's hopeful eyes, I always looked to the best in him, which began to manifest as he bloomed into a mature, compassionate young man in his last two years of high school. I had to smile when I read these lines of Steindl-Rast:

Hope looks at all things the way a mother looks at her child, with a *passion for the possible*. But that way of looking is creative. It creates the space in which perfection can unfold. More than that, the eyes of hope look through all imperfections to the heart of all things and find it perfect (italics added; *Gratefulness, The Heart of Prayer,* p. 142).

Put this way, hope is really a form of blessing. To bless is to increase, to allow something to unfold in its fullness. To hope is to create a sacred space, a space of possibility, in which the goodness of the Universe can express itself. The stance we adopt in that sacred space is one of readiness, openness and non-attachment to a particular outcome. In his classic *The Revolution of Hope,* Erich Fromm defines the patient, wise waiting of hope in a magnificent metaphor:

> Hope . . . is neither passive waiting nor is it unrealistic forcing of circumstances that cannot occur. It is like the crouched tiger, which will jump only when the moment for jumping has come. . . . To hope means to be ready at every moment for that which is not yet born, and yet not become desperate if there is no birth in our lifetime (p. 9).

In the chapters that follow we will consider the time-honored methods of meditation, contemplation and prayer, whose practice fosters hope: the willingness to listen patiently for the inner voice that will bring us to the path of freedom, and courage—opening the eyes of the heart that most clearly see the way.

PART THREE

Practices for Awakening to the Sacred

Ask and it shall be given you;
Seek, and you shall find;
Knock, and it shall be opened to you.

For whoever asks, receives; and
he who seeks, finds; and to him who
knocks, the door is opened.

Jesus, in Matthew 7:7, 8

CHAPTER NINE
Meditation and Centering Prayer

It is only with the heart that one can see rightly; what is essential is invisible to the eye.

Antoine de Saint-Exupéry, *The Little Prince*

Just after Christmas 1990 I received a letter from a young man I know. It was written from a Boston-area hospital where he was being treated for an intestinal illness called Crohn's disease. Fritz wanted to share a puzzling experience with me that had occurred a few days earlier. He viewed it as a spiritual experience. The hospital psychiatrist viewed it as a chemical imbalance related to his treatment. Fritz and I met shortly after he was released from the hospital, and he told me the following story.

Fritz was sitting in bed when he suddenly felt a strong bolt of energy rush up his spine. Although Western medical science and psychology has no explanation for such events, Eastern science and psychology does. The body's subtle energy is called chi in China, ki in Japan, kundalini in India. It is the energy that flows in acupuncture meridians and is stored in reservoirs known as chakras. Perhaps you remember having an "aha" experience and feeling a chill go up your spine. If so you have felt the rising of this subtle energy, which accompanies sudden "knowings" and opens a deeper level of perception, not through the physical senses but through the spiritual senses, the eyes of the heart.

Fritz's spiritual sight suddenly opened with the jolt of uprushing energy. There he was, sitting in his hospital bed seeing the same things he had seen for days with his physical eyes, but seeing them in an entirely new way. He spoke of observing the nurses hurrying by with carts of pills and injections, but from his expanded perspective he *knew* at the deepest level of his being that everything was perfect. *Everything that was happening was perfect*. Think about that for a minute. Have you ever had a realization that the whole beautiful, terrible crazy drama of life was perfect? Sometimes this realization comes during holy moments, those brief suspensions of time when eternity steals over us and we feel the inherent integrity of life.

Fritz entered this state in an unusual setting for a holy moment— hospitalized with high-calorie feeding solution dripping into his veins. Suspended in the state of perfection, Fritz also had a realization of his own inner purity. Think about that! How might it feel to know that despite all the mistakes you have made, despite all the times you have felt foolish, unworthy, bad, or just plain "not enough," you suddenly saw that your core self was perfect, worthy, pure and without blemish. This is the experience of seeing or realizing the Higher Self, the true nature of who we are.

If you have not had such an experience personally—and most of us have not—it may be difficult to understand. When Fritz shared his experience with me, his eyes were lighted and his face was soft. He exuded the purity he had experienced and an extraordinary humility.

Through a fascinating serendipity I knew exactly what Fritz meant, not just empathetically, but because I had experienced precisely the same state in 1989 as part of a religious ceremony presided over by a South American shaman. We had been given a drink of the extract from the Ayahuasca vine, a woody root that many native peoples have used as part of their religious observances for thousands of years. The extract contains a visionary substance that opens a doorway into the imaginal realm of First Stories and direct perception of the sacred.

At first the Ayahuasca made me nauseated and restless, but after about twenty minutes I settled down and closed my eyes. I became aware of the movement of fantastic streams of energy within my body. The experience was multisensorial. I felt the energy, saw it as light and color, and heard it as indescribably beautiful music. Like Fritz, I felt the kundalini rise. It started from the base of my spine and moved up into my belly. While I have heard the term "fire in the belly," I had never experienced it before. The energy was a powerful, fierce kind of courage, more like a fire in my soul. It was an absolute confidence and certainty that I had a purpose in this life, that I was in tune with it and that I would have all the help I needed in fulfilling that purpose. When the energy reached my heart I was, for lack of better words, "shown" inside my own soul. I wept uncontrollably at the realization that it was perfectly pure.

Although all the ancient scriptures assure the reader that the essential Self is pure and without stain, it is hard to imagine how it feels to actually experience that truth. Rather than seeing with the eyes of the heart (from the viewpoint of the Self) most of us see with the eyes of the ego (focusing on faults and fears). So, as you might imagine, the sudden realization of purity is a dramatic shift in perception. For a few moments while Fritz and I recalled our experiences, I perceived life once again through the eyes of the heart, sensing the perfection in all things. The Isa-Upanishad says, "He who perceives all beings as the Self, for him how can there be delusion or grief, when he sees this oneness everywhere?"[1]

I was intrigued as Fritz continued to describe his experience because the next step also paralleled my own. Following the realization of his purity and the absolute perfection of all things, he began to notice his ego. The ego is that part of ourself that thinks it is separate from the Whole. Like a frightened child, terrified of abandonment, the ego projects fear and guilt to maintain its own seeming control over events. In this way, the ego maintains the illusion of safety at the price of separation from Self, others and the divine.

It is a fascinating experience to become aware of the essential, pure

[1] In his translation and commentary on *The Upanishads,* Swami Paramananda says of this verse: "He who perceives the Self everywhere never shrinks from anything, because through his higher consciousness he feels united with all life. When a man sees God in all beings and all beings in God, and also God dwelling in his own Soul, how can he hate any living thing? Grief and delusion rest upon a belief in diversity, which leads to competition and all forms of selfishness. With the realization of oneness, the sense of diversity vanishes and the cause of misery is removed."

Self and the ego at the same time. The ego might step in and say, "This is all crazy, you are not pure," and then rerun your mistakes or take you on a journey through fear. During my kundalini experience I discovered that I could notice the tricks of the ego and just keep letting go and moving back into the purity. This striking movement back and forth from ego to Self occurs more subtly throughout our waking hours as we cycle through times when we are relaxed and focused in the present to times when we feel stuck in past and future doubts and fears. Developing the ability to *observe*, to become *aware* of, these normal shifts in consciousness is the beginning of learning to make the voluntary shift from ego to Self.

The practice of meditation is the oldest known method for sidestepping the ego and learning to see with the eyes of the heart—the Self—but it also has a variety of other applications: medical, psychological and spiritual. Because of its many facets, a bewildering array of meditation practices exist aimed at promoting different, although related, outcomes. A good guide to the diversity of meditation practices is found in Daniel Goleman's book *The Meditative Mind*.

Later in the chapter I will share some simple meditative practices with you. But before we come to the practicalities of meditation, let's consider some of the technicalities.

MEDITATION AND THE RELAXATION RESPONSE

Technically, meditation is *intentional concentration on a selected focus*. That focus may be either secular or nonsecular. In a secular sense, when absorbed intensely in any activity we have a tendency to lose track of time and tune out extraneous stimuli like telephones, doorbells or voices. When I write, for example, my family jokes that the house could burn down and I would keep on writing, blissfully unaware of what was going on around me. Perhaps you have become so absorbed in gardening, reading or even balancing your checkbook that your breathing slowed and you became as single-pointed as a panther stalking her dinner! In this state creativity flowers, intuition leads to a deeper wisdom, the natural healing system of the body is engaged, our best physical and mental potential manifests itself and we feel psychologically satisfied. These are the fruits of secular meditation, whether it occurs naturally or through the specific intent to meditate on an activity like walking, exercising, observing natural beauty or mentally focusing on a repetitive mental stimulus while sitting with closed eyes.

I originally took up secular meditation for its medical benefits and in time discovered its deeper psychological and spiritual benefits. As I recounted in *Minding the Body, Mending the Mind,* I began to meditate in the late 1960s out of desperation when a seemingly endless array of stress-related illnesses—including migraine headache, irritable bowel syndrome, high blood pressure, chronic bronchitis, anxiety attacks, immune dysfunction and dizzy spells—failed to respond to the best of conventional medical treatment.

A graduate student in medical sciences at Harvard Medical School at the time, I had access to excellent physicians. The cure for my ills, however, was not to be found in medication. It lay instead in learning to let go of the ego's perfectionism and insecurity that was the root of my "stress" and the source of disruption for my nervous system.

My nervous system was like a car that idled too high, always on the ready to respond to a threat. Since practically every interaction with another human being seemed threatening, my nervous system was in chronic overreaction to life. I learned to use simple breathing and meditation techniques to decrease the arousal of my nervous system, techniques that I discuss in detail in *Minding the Body, Mending the Mind*. Within six months of beginning a regular meditation practice, all my physical symptoms had disappeared, an outcome that seemed like a miracle at the time.

The physiological benefits of meditation were first studied scientifically by Herbert Benson, M.D., and R. Keith Wallace, Ph.D. They found that transcendental meditation, which involves focusing on a mantra—or sacred sound—decreased heart rate, breathing rate and oxygen consumption. These changes were accompanied by reproducible hormonal alterations and an increase in alpha waves in the cerebral cortex. They described these restful, restorative changes as a "wakeful hypometabolic state," which Benson subsequently termed the relaxation response, the physiological antagonist of the fight-or-flight response. Benson went on to show that any simple kind of concentration meditation, whether secular or nonsecular, produced the same core of healthful bodily changes.

More recent research shows that under some conditions deficient immune functions such as natural killer-cell activity (lymphocytes that patrol the body for virus-infected or cancer cells) and helper T-cell function (lymphocytes that help the immune system form antibodies against invading bacteria, parasites and fungi) can be significantly restored by such easy-to-practice forms of meditation as progressive muscle relaxation. Importantly, these beneficial changes occur after only a few weeks of meditation, even in novice meditators who are almost always convinced that they are not doing the meditation correctly. When I ask people at workshops how many meditate, for example, a significant number usually raise their hands. When I ask how many people think they are meditating "well," most of the hands go down.

Most people find that the mind is a very busy place, jumping from thought to thought like a wild monkey. People typically lose their focus and get lost in thought, only to "come to" a minute or two later and think, "Uh oh, I was supposed to be meditating." This is absolutely natural. Every time you let go of thinking and return to your chosen focus of concentration, the mental muscles of awareness are being exercised. Remarkably, even when most of a meditation period is spent thinking, beneficial bodily changes still occur. When meditation is discontinued, those changes generally disappear within a few weeks.

The relaxation response induced by meditation has proven useful as a medical treatment for a wide range of stress-related disorders and chronic pain. Jon Kabat-Zinn, Ph.D., a colleague of mine at the University of Massachusetts Medical Center in Worcester, Massachusetts, developed a well-researched clinical program based on a form of meditation called mindfulness. In his book *Full Catastrophe Living,* Dr. Kabat-Zinn explains how the ancient practice of mindfulness—or moment-to-moment awareness of what is—can reduce chronic pain and alleviate a variety of physical disorders.

Pain reduction is accomplished not only by the physiological effects of the meditation, but also by mental changes that mindfulness trains.

Mindfulness practice encourages the development of an observing awareness that notices pain without becoming emotionally involved in it. Being the observer of the pain (whether physical or emotional) is an entirely different state than being the victim of the pain. The result of this shift is a reduction in suffering and a disruption of the vicious cycle of helplessness, anger and tension that pain can sustain. Dr. Kabat-Zinn's stress-reduction and relaxation program was an inspiration and early model for the Mind/Body Clinic that I cofounded in 1980 and then directed until 1988 at two different teaching hospitals of the Harvard Medical School. *Minding the Body, Mending the Mind* is based on our experiences at the clinic and focuses predominantly on the physical and psychological aspects of concentration meditation, mindfulness and creative imagination.

I received a letter recently from a man who had read that earlier book and enjoyed it thoroughly, although he felt I was "holding something back." He subsequently read *Guilt Is the Teacher, Love Is the Lesson* and found that the spirituality that had been implicit in my first book was made explicit in the second. Minding the body and mending the mind rest on the deeper ground of mending our relation to the spirit, both our own individual soul and the Universal Spirit of which we are all a part. Through the years many of my patients, like myself, have begun a meditation practice for its effect on the body and continued it because of its progressive healing of the soul and opening to the spirit.

MEDITATION, MIND AND SPIRIT

The medieval Spanish mystic, poet and theologian Saint John of the Cross taught that *interior silence—the inner stillness to which meditation leads—is where the Spirit "secretly anoints the soul and heals our deepest wounds."*

In this sense meditation is a form of spiritual psychotherapy that I believe complements, but does not replace, secular psychotherapy. Sometimes even after we understand our pasts, the pain still persists. Meditation invites us to let go of old pain and to heal. Part of that healing involves a discovery of the inner purity—of the divine beloved that dwells both within and beyond us—that Fritz and I both experienced.

Saint John of the Cross said,

> You ask, "Since He whom my soul loves is within me, why don't I find or experience him?" The Beloved is concealed. Your Bridegroom is like a treasure hidden in a field, for which the merchant sold all his possessions (Mt 13:44), and that field is your soul. In order to find Him you should forget all your possessions and creatures and hide in the interior, secret chambers of your spirit.[2]

This forgetting of all your "possessions and creatures" is a challenging task that is magnified at times when our minds are drawn to contemplate something other than the chosen focus of our meditation. For example, after nearly two decades of married life (and meditation) I decided to redecorate the living room. I had never actually decorated a room from scratch before. Instead, our furnishings had always been an eclectic collection of hand-me-downs, garage sale finds and treasures salvaged from the town dump, a style my mother dubbed "Early Morgan Memorial" after a chain of thrift shops famous in Massachusetts.

For weeks visions of chairs, sofas, coffee tables, pictures, budgets and plans danced before my eyes during meditation. I mentally redecorated my husband's tropical fishtanks. Oriental rugs floated in and out of my consciousness. I would notice my attachment to these possessions and let go, only to find window shades dancing by a few breaths later. Interior silence awaited at a level of mind much deeper than the surface desire to acquire and possess. During the redecoration period I often had to meditate for fifteen or twenty minutes to finish thinking about the living-room decor, and let go and enter a deeper place of relative interior silence.

And Saint John's "creatures"? Fear, anger, blame, shame and other strong emotions are the creatures that typically surface in meditation to remind us of what we are holding onto that needs healing. Unfin-

---

[2]From *Meditations with John of the Cross*, a centering book by Camille Campbell, p. 64.

ished business tends to float up as soon as the mind quiets down. Since many people are used to avoiding themselves through workaholism, TV, alcohol, drugs or anything that keeps the mind busy or numb, meditation is a time when all the things we may have hoped to push away can come crowding in. "Wow, she's sitting down with nothing to distract her!" And here come the harpies.

Perhaps, as I have done, you have sat to meditate and found yourself remembering some old or new anger. If you try to deny it or push it away—"Oh, no, I'm not supposed to feel angry now. This anger is ruining my peace"—or if you welcome and explore it looking for insight—"This must be a leftover of my childhood feelings about my mother. I have internalized her critical nature and am projecting it"—then you engage the anger, and it becomes the focus of your meditation.

How, then, do you approach these powerful "creatures" that guard the way to the heart? The Buddhists say that one doesn't quiet a raging bull by corralling it but by releasing it into a spacious pasture. The idea is to let the mind become spacious around the bull—in this case, angry thoughts—by acknowledging the anger and letting it go, refocusing on whatever your object of meditative concentration may be. If you had an insight about the anger, wait until after the meditation to investigate it. If it is important, you will remember it; if it isn't, you won't. Some of the clearest instructions on how to deal with thoughts, where to focus the mind and how to think about the process of meditation are given in the practice of centering prayer.

CENTERING PRAYER—BECOMING PRESENT TO THE DIVINE

The single best book I have read about meditation was written by Father Thomas Keating, a Cistercian priest, monk and abbot who currently resides at St. Benedict's monastery in Snowmass, Colorado. He is one of the founders of the centering prayer movement. After many years of practicing different forms of meditation I settled into the practice of centering prayer, which I also like to teach because of its clarity, simplicity and effectiveness.

Centering prayer is a form of meditation in which the object of focus is the divine presence. In many other forms of meditation—such as Eastern practices, Judeo-Christian practices and the more physically oriented practice of the "relaxation response"—the focus is generally on a word or phrase. The focus phrase or mantra may be repeated either in rhythm with the breathing, as suggested by Dr. Herbert Benson in *The Relaxation Response,* or without reference to breathing, as in transcendental meditation, as taught by the Maharishi Mahesh Yogi.

Centering prayer differs from most forms of concentration meditation because, although it involves the repetition of a sacred word chosen by the meditator, its focus is not on the sacred word per se, but on inner silence. The word—which can be as simple as "peace," "shalom," "Jesus," "let go" or any other pleasing focus—is not repeated continually, but only as a reminder to return to the silence when the mind begins to wander. The word is sacred, says Keating, not because of its own characteristics, but because it strengthens our intent to remain in God's presence:

> The word is a sacred word because *it is the symbol of your intention to open yourself to the mystery of God's presence beyond thoughts, images or emotions. It is chosen not for its content but for its intent.* It is merely a pointer that expresses the direction of your inward movement toward the presence of God (italics added; p. 110).

The *process* of centering prayer, which involves using the sacred word as a pointer toward interior stillness, is *itself* the prayer, regardless of the word repeated. Like most types of formal meditation, it involves sitting in a quiet place, closing your eyes, relaxing your body and focusing your attention.

Some people can access interior stillness by focusing on the silence that is inherently present in any place. *(Close your eyes right now, take a couple of letting-go breaths—big sighs—and take a minute to listen for the silence that is present beyond any sounds.)* If you entered the silence, chances are that thoughts began to intrude upon it before a minute was even up. In centering prayer, you would repeat your sacred word to remind you to let go of thoughts and return to the silence.

Some people enter the silence by repeating the sacred word until the mind quiets. Then, as before, the sacred word is again repeated whenever the mind wanders.

I have a favorite way of coming into the divine presence. I close my eyes and take a minute or two to remember a "holy moment" when I felt present to nature, myself, a pet or another person. I savor the sights, sounds, fragrances and inner feelings of peace, love and connectedness that the memory evokes. I then let go of the memory and bask in the divine presence that remains, using the sacred word, as it is intended, to bring me back into silence when my mind wanders off.

Regardless of the technique you use to enter the silence, you will slip out of it soon enough. Your mind will start to question, doubt, evaluate, criticize, comment and otherwise pull you out of oneness. Meditation is like a form of mental martial arts because you learn to sidestep the mind and glide back to the silence. This is what repeating a sacred word helps you to do.

Whenever the mind begins to wander, the idea is to go back to the sacred word, reminding yourself of your intent to dwell in the oneness of the Self. Keating advises:

> When you become aware that you are thinking some other thought, return to the sacred word as the expression of your intent. The effectiveness of this prayer does not depend on how distinctly you say the sacred word or how often, *but rather on the gentleness with which you introduce it into your imagination in the beginning and the promptness* with which you return to it when you are hooked on some other thought.
>
> Thoughts are an inevitable part of centering prayer. Our ordinary thoughts are like boats sitting on a river so closely packed together that we cannot see the river that is holding them up. *A "thought" in the context of this prayer is any perception that crosses the inner screen of consciousness.* We are normally aware of one object after another passing

across the inner screen of consciousness: images, memories, feelings, external impressions. When we slow down
that flow for a little while, space begins to appear between
the boats. Up comes the reality on which they were floating
(italics added; *ibid.*).

The process of meditation, so simply and elegantly described by
Keating, *is a shift in awareness away from the thoughts that float
on the river of consciousness to the river itself.* That river is the
divine presence. This is the essential reframe of meditation. Instead
of identifying our life with the succession of boats (thoughts) that go
down the river, we begin to identify it as the river. As we do so, the
reality that the boats are transient but the river is ever-present comes
into focus, and our perception about what is real and what is unreal
shifts.

Notice how Keating defines thought: any perception that crosses
the inner screen of consciousness. What to do with these thoughts?
The instruction is always the same: Pay as little attention as possible
to them, whether they are of the usual laundry list variety of to-do's
and random associations, emotions, bodily sensations, streams of
attractive or repulsive imagery, or seemingly earth-shattering insights and revelations. A subtle type of thinking that Keating clarifies
is self-reflection.

As you settle into deep peace and freedom from particular
thoughts, a desire to reflect on what is happening may arise.
You may think, "At last I am getting some place!" or, "This
feeling is just great!" or "If only I could make a mental note
of how I got here so that I can get back whenever I want!"
... You are being offered a choice between reflecting on
what is going on and letting go of the experience. If you let
go, you go deeper into interior silence. If you reflect, you
come out and have to start over. There will be a lot of
starting over (p. 12).

Keating goes on to make the point that being in the divine presence
is like breathing. We can have all the air we want as long as we don't

try to possess it and hang onto it! At some point, you may let go into the stillness and then everything disappears, including the sacred word. What happens in this space is variable. Like deep sleep, you may lose awareness altogether and move out of time. You may have an experience like Fritz and I did. You may enter the Light. In the meantime, Keating's directions are delightfully clear: "Resist no thought, hang on to no thought, react emotionally to no thought. Whatever image, feeling, reflection or experience attracts your attention, return to the sacred word."

This type of meditation is uncomplicated, and the instructions are clear. It is suitable both for the beginner and for the person who has been meditating for a lifetime. The simple practice of letting go will help you become aware of the presence of the divine in nature, in yourself and in other people. The love and joy that are inherent in Spirit—that are the very essence of Spirit—will begin to permeate your life. Where love and joy exist as the ground of your being, pain and fear can exist only transiently, as boats floating down the river. And in those times when our attention is fixed on those boats, we will have the courage and hope to understand the words of King Solomon: "This, too, shall pass."

A SIMPLE PRACTICE OF MEDITATION

1. Set and setting. Sit in a quiet, comfortable place that feels peaceful and inviting. The right atmosphere draws you automatically into the divine presence. In warm weather I meditate outdoors by a little pond that we dug in our backyard and stocked with koi (Japanese goldfish) and tadpoles who duly metamorphosed into twanging bullfrogs. The reflections on the water, the smell of the earth and the changing scenery as spring mellows into summer and summer turns to fall are a wonderful backdrop to meditation.

Our current home is large enough that I finally have a place reserved specifically for meditation when the weather is inhospitable. In previous years I have used the top of a bureau, a corner of the kitchen, a nook in the hall. Several years ago I took the doors off a closet in my study and painted the triangular-shaped interior a flat white.

The walls are adorned with pictures of babies, friends, family members, pets and assorted saints. What the pictures have in common is the inner state of the people and animals. They all project love or joy. I usually spend a few minutes looking into these beautiful faces before I begin. In the center of the space there is a low table with a variety of meaningful objects that change over the years. One of them is a large stone that weighs about two pounds and is shaped remarkably like a female breast, complete with a pigmented areola and nipple. My dear friend, Celia Thaxter Hubbard, found the stone on a beach many years ago and gave it to me as a remembrance of the Great Mother. Along with a sandalwood box containing the rose that was on my mother's pillow when she died, the stone evokes the divine feminine.

A light-gray stone in which a perfect dark-gray heart is set is a reminder of the continuity of this life with unseen worlds. When young Mathew Hitchcock died in the summer of 1990, I walked the beach two days after his passing. I felt a presence and thought, "If that's you, Mat, give me a sign that you are all right." I looked down and saw the heart stone. A bowl of rose petals that our woman's group sprinkled me with before I went off on tour with *Guilt Is the Teacher, Love Is the Lesson,* a wooden heart carved by a friend and given to Myrin and me for a wedding present, a tiny silver Buddha that friends sent from Thailand and a jar of sacred ash from India are touchstones that evoke love, connectedness and gratitude. A candle, an incense holder and a chalice complete my sacred space.

Even if there is no place you can count on as your own, you can keep a "medicine bag" full of your own touchstones. When you are ready to meditate, arrange the items as you wish; when you finish, pack them up again! Some people like to light incense or to "smudge" (ritual cleansing from the Native American tradition) their meditation space with cedar or sage. Do whatever makes you happy and brings the sacred to mind. But remember that whatever ritual you construct is for your own benefit, not to woo God. The Cosmic Birther is already present.

2. Letting go. Wherever you have chosen to meditate, begin by closing your eyes and stretching. Take a few letting-go breaths. If you are

tense, do a brief progressive muscle relaxation. When you feel your body begin to relax, check your posture. It is easiest to meditate if the spine is straight and the body posture is symmetrical.

3. Connecting with the Higher Self. From time to time each of us experiences "holy moments" when we make an automatic shift out of thinking into being. I recall a trip to the Hawaiian island of Kauai, where we spent part of a crystal-clear afternoon ocean kayaking. The water was azure blue, the sun was warm and a gentle breeze carried the subtle fragrance of flowers. Our bodies were rocked by the ocean rhythm, and we responded to that rhythm by dipping our oars and cooperating with the tides in an easy forward flow. Every cell in my body felt vibrantly alive and at one with the sky, the sea and God. I was filled with peace, joy, awe and gratitude—attributes of the Higher Self. For a moment I had stopped thinking and become present to the divine.

Bringing back such a memory when you were in tune with life— present to beauty, to another person, to a creative moment, to a pet—connects you to your Higher Self and to the divine presence, which are one. This is an excellent start to centering prayer because it brings you into an immediate awareness of the inner silence. If you want to try this exercise, tape these instructions for yourself or have a friend read them to you. Make sure to pause long enough at the dotted areas to carry out the instructions. After you have tried this once, you can do it on your own any time, drawing on the library of special memories that you may not have thought about for years. This "holy moment" exercise is wonderful not only as a preliminary to centering prayer or other forms of meditation, but as a meditation in its own right:

> *Take a nice, slow stretch. Now close your eyes and take a few letting-go breaths, like big sighs of relief. . . . . . Notice what it feels like to breathe, how your body rises up slightly as you breathe in and settles back as you breathe out. . . . . . Enjoy the sensation of breath moving in and out, feeling its natural rhythm . . . . . . feeling how each outbreath is an opportunity to let go to the deepest part of*

*your being . . . . . . to the storehouse of your own special
memories. . . . . . Remember a holy moment . . . . . . a time
when you felt deeply connected to life . . . . . . watching a
sunset . . . . . . creating something of beauty . . . . . . deeply
in touch with another person . . . . . . loving a pet . . . . . .
feeling present to life. . . . . .*

*If more than one memory comes to mind, choose one
and relive it in as much detail as you like. . . . . . What do
you see around you, above and below you?. . . . . . What
are the colors and the shapes of things?. . . . . . Are there
any sounds?. . . . . . What about fragrances?. . . . . . What
are the textures of the things around you? Are you touching
or being touched by anything?. . . . . . Is there a
breeze?. . . . . . Can you feel the earth under your
feet?. . . . . . How does the memory feel in your
body?. . . . . .*

*Let the memory fade and focus on the peaceful feelings
that remain.*

4. The sacred word. Choose a sacred word. If you feel connected to
the Eastern tradition you might enjoy the Sanskrit *hamsa* mantra,
which means "I am that," a proclamation of oneness with the divine,
or *om nama shivaya,* which means "I honor the Self in all." Hebrew,
like Sanskrit, is an excellent focus for meditation because the words
themselves resonate in our bodies and awaken our memories. *Shalom*, meaning "peace," and *shem*, meaning "light," are both beautiful
and evocative words for meditation.

Neil Douglas-Klotz, in *Prayers for the Cosmos: Meditations on the
Aramaic Words of Jesus,* suggests a number of sacred words in Jesus'
original Hebraic language, Aramaic. The word *abwoon*, which Jesus
used for God and which is usually translated as "Father," is more
properly translated as "Birther, Father-Mother of the Cosmos." I love
to feel the word *abwoon* in my body. Sometimes I use it during the
day, for a moment or two, as a breath mantra. I breath in and repeat
aaah, bringing God into my body. I breath out and repeat *bwooooooon*,
feeling God's breath moving through my body and resonating in my
cells. In centering prayer one does not focus on the breathing, so for

that purpose one would just repeat *abwoon* without reference to the breath.

Secular words like "thank you," "peace," "love," "beauty," "harmony," "oneness" or any other attribute of the Higher Self also make good sacred words. Choose any word or words (but keep it short) that are sacred to you, remembering that the magic really isn't in the words, but in your intent to use them to direct you into the sacred presence of God.

5. **Establishing a practice.** Meditation is a habit. In order to form most habits, you need to repeat a behavior until it becomes second nature. Choosing a consistent time of day for meditation and making a commitment to do it daily is the easiest way to get started and to keep going. It is best to practice for a minimum of twenty minutes. The longer you sit, the more you will be drawn into silence. It often takes fifteen minutes before the mind even begins to quiet down, so the longer you sit the more silence you are likely to experience. But if ten minutes is all you have on a given day, ten minutes are much better than no minutes! Good times to practice are early morning before the day begins, and in the early evening before supper. But any time will do unless you are exhausted (you are likely to fall asleep), you have just eaten a big meal (you are likely to fall asleep), or you have just had a couple of cups of coffee (you are likely to feel antsy).

While many people profit from a regular practice of sitting meditation, it is by no means the only way to remember the sacred. As we will discuss in the next chapter, washing the dishes can be a meditation, as can petting the cat. My all-time favorite meditation is a small, moist piece of chocolate cake eaten with exquisite attention and tremendous gratitude. Any time that we are fully present in the moment, we are meditating. We are free from the limitations of thought and at one with the river of life.

CHAPTER TEN
How Do We Talk to God?

Do our prayers come true? The answer lies in the way that we pray. Let's pray in a way that our prayers are true.

Ainsley Meares, M.D.

The bedtime prayer I learned as a small child was: "Now I lay me down to sleep, I pray the Lord my soul to keep. If I should die before I wake, I pray the Lord my soul to take."

Reciting this little ditty filled me with horror. I could hardly stand to close my eyes, wondering how often God took the souls of little children while they slept. There were actually two worrisome parts to prayer. First, I might die. Second, God might not take my soul. What then? What happened to the souls of little children that didn't find their way home? Did they wander endlessly in the dark, or were they gobbled up by evil spirits? I decided that prayer was not for me. It ruined my peace of mind.

When I went to a wonderful camp for Jewish girls at eight years of age, my ideas about prayer began to change. The bedtime prayer at Camp Pembroke was a sweet, spiritual rendition of taps sung by Hadassah Blocker, the camp director. As the twilight deepened in the summer stillness, all the campers crawled into their cots. The PA system would then switch on with a crackle and Hadassah's warm, throaty voice would float through the semicircle of little white bunk houses: "Day is done, gone the sun, from the lake, from the hills, from the sky. All is well, rest in peace, God is nigh."

The lilting melody and Hadassah's words reassured me of God's presence and created a holy moment every night. I would fall asleep wrapped in the cocoon of God's love, sure of my safety, filled with joy and peace. Do our prayers come true? As the late psychiatrist and mystic Ainsley Meares said, "Let's pray in a way that our prayers *are* true." Rather than worrying about where my soul would go at death, at Camp Pembroke I learned to use prayer as an affirmation of living in the divine presence now.

HOW DO WE PRAY?

The cover article of the January 6, 1992, *Newsweek* was entitled "Talking to God." The secret communion with our creator is not so secret any longer. The article cited statistics from the National Opinion Research Council about the prayer life of what *Newsweek* called "allegedly rootless, materialistic, self-centered" Americans. Seventy-eight percent of all Americans report praying at least weekly, while 57 percent say that they pray daily. Studies indicate that the majority of people begin to pray in earnest after the age of thirty, when "the illusion that we are masters of our own fate fades and adults develop a deeper need to call on the Master of the Universe."

According to a poll by Paloma and Gallup on "varieties of prayer," the way that we pray also changes with age. Rather than praying for material gain, as we mature we are more likely to pray in the hope of experiencing God's presence. Thus 45 percent of eighteen- to twenty-four-year-olds who pray do so meditatively, whereas 70 percent of sixty-five-year-olds engage in meditative prayers. Centering prayer, as we discussed in the last chapter, is an excellent method of experiencing the divine presence.

While centering prayer originated in the Christian tradition, the idea that prayer is the way we enter God's presence is also a tenet of Judaism. The Hasidic rabbi Pinchas of Koretz taught that "prayer is not to God, prayer is God" and that "all of your prayers should be for the sake of the Presence who herself is called prayer." If you are interested in learning more about the Jewish tradition of contemplative prayer, you may enjoy *Your Word Is Fire: The Hasidic Masters on Contemplative Prayer*, edited and translated by Arthur Green and Barry H. Holtz. (Actually, centering prayer is entirely ecumenical in application.)

PRAYING FOR

Centering and contemplative prayer are a kind of attunement to God's presence—a praying with—that are their own answer. But what about the practice of praying for? Sometimes we pray for health, for help, for material or spiritual sustenance for ourselves or for others. Are these prayers answered? Many people have approached me at seminars and sent me anecdotes about the power of prayer in recovery from illness. One of the most touching stories of this type concerned Brian, a little boy I met in December 1991 on a Geraldo Rivera Christmas show about miracles, for which I was the so-called expert. (It was fun being an expert on miracles!)

The healthy, active four-year-old I sat next to on that show bore little resemblance to the heart-rending pictures they showed of the small child whose third liver transplant was failing and who had developed a transplant-related pneumonia that is usually fatal. The doctors had told Brian's family that there was nothing more they could do for the child. But Brian's mother wasn't ready to give up. She arranged for the local newspaper to print a story about her son along with her urgent request that readers pray for him. They estimated that 40,000 people prayed for the child. The day after the article appeared, Brian began a rapid and unexpected recovery that earned him the hospital's title of their little "Easter Miracle."

Indeed, there is a small medical literature on the efficacy of prayer. Stimulated by the accounts of patients who claimed to have been helped by prayer, and out of his own faith, cardiologist Randolph Byrd conducted an excellent clinical study on the effects of prayer at a distance while he was on staff at the San Francisco General Hospital. Published in July 1988 in the *Southern Medical Journal*, this randomized, controlled double-blind study (the gold-standard of clinical studies) proved that prayer helped patients with heart attacks to recover. Byrd randomly assigned more than 400 patients admitted to the coronary intensive care unit with heart attacks to either standard medical care or standard care plus prayer at a distance through prayer groups.

Neither the patients nor the staff knew who was being prayed for, eliminating the possibility that the prayed-for patients might get preferential treatment or heal through the placebo effect (the belief that prayer might help). Those who were prayed for had fewer cardiac arrests, were less likely to need mechanical ventilation (respirators), had a much reduced incidence of pulmonary edema (fluid in the lungs), suffered fewer infections and needed less medication. Without doubt, many of the patients in the control group were also being prayed for, but those in the prayer group got an extra measure of attention.

There is a nonsectarian foundation in Salem, Oregon, called Spindrift whose purpose is to carry out experiments on the efficacy of prayer. They publish a newsletter and make the results of their experiments available to the public. If you are interested in such research, Spindrift is listed in the Resources section at the end of this book. You can also read an excellent review of the Spindrift studies in Dr. Larry Dossey's fine book *Recovering the Soul*, which outlines the Spindrift findings on the most effective ways to pray.

As Dr. Dossey reports, the Spindrift research is based on their underlying assumption that all of us have "divine attributes, a qualitative oneness with God." In their early research, Spindrift investigated the power of prayer to restore vitality to seeds that were poisoned by being soaked in salt water. The seeds were planted in a shallow container of vermiculite, divided by a string into side A and side B. Following prayer for one side or the other, the seedlings were counted. In many repetitions of the study, the prayed-for side sprouted significantly more seedlings than the "untreated" side.

One of the most intriguing questions that the Spindrift studies addressed concerns the effects of "directed" versus "nondirected" prayer. In Dr. Dossey's words, "Is prayer more effective if a specific goal is held in the mind, or does a simple, 'Thy will be done' approach work better?" The results are striking. Both types of prayer proved effective in stimulating the germination and growth of the seeds, but the "Thy will be done" approach was more than twice as effective as specifying a specific desired outcome. As a result of these studies, Spindrift suggests that we pray by holding in our minds a "pure and holy" consciousness of whomever or whatever we are praying for. They call this method genuine spiritual healing and contrast it to faith healing and other methods that rely on directed prayer.

Metaphysicians from Christian and Eastern schools of thought agree with Spindrift researchers that essentially holding a person in the Light and praying that their wholeness be manifest is an effective form of prayer. This type of prayer does not specify an outcome. It does not demand that a sick person be made well or that a poor person become rich. If only blesses the person with wholeness in the understanding that our sight is too narrow to know what a person requires for their wholeness, but that God certainly knows.

If poverty, illness, divorce, addiction or any other form of pain is a karmic finishing of events, it would be sad to think that we could deprive ourselves or another person of growth through misguided prayers. This, it would seem, does not happen. Prayers that are not karmically harmonious are ineffective. It is no wonder, then, that the great teachers of all traditions tell us not to pray for the cessation of pain but for the courage to endure whatever suffering we must traverse on the way to freedom, and for the ability to live our lives in harmony with the divine will:

> *Lord, we pray not for tranquility, not that our tribulations may cease; we pray for Thy Spirit and Thy love that thou grant us strength and grace to overcome adversity.*

> Savonarola

> *Bring this life into harmony with Divine purpose. . . . May this life come into harmony with God's Will. May you so live that all who meet you will be uplifted, that all who*

*bless you will be blessed, that all who serve you will receive
the greatest satisfaction. If any should attempt to harm
you, may they contact your thought of God and be healed.*

Peace Pilgrim

*Let me not pray to be sheltered from dangers but to be
fearless in facing them. Let me not beg for the stilling of
my pain but for the heart to conquer it.*

Rabindranath Tagore

PRAYER AS BLESSING—
LOVING-KINDNESS MEDITATION

The Spindrift understanding that "all of us have divine attributes,
a qualitative oneness with God" affirms our roles as emergent co-
creators who spread the Light of the One through blessing, which
literally means "increasing."

My favorite form of blessing comes from the Buddhist tradition
and is called *metta*, or loving-kindness meditation. The traditional
blessings include phrases such as, "May all beings be peaceful," "May
all beings be happy," "May all beings be free from affliction." You
can expand on these blessings in whatever way moves you. Stephen
Levine, a therapist and Buddhist teacher who, along with his wife,
Ondrea, has worked for many years with the dying, suggests that we
repeat these blessings first for ourselves, then for our loved ones,
then for those who we may be in conflict with and finally for all
beings. You might enjoy repeating loving-kindness blessings, as I
often do, as part of your meditation practice or prayer life. Levine
suggests that some people might even enjoy *metta* as their primary
meditation practice.

The following meditation consists of an introduction to bring ourselves into the presence of the Light and into our own hearts, followed
by the traditional loving-kindness blessings. You might want to do
the entire meditation or skip directly to the blessings. You can tape
this meditation for yourself, adding music if you like. Be sure to leave

adequate space at the dots to carry out each instruction. Use the pronoun "him" or "her" as appropriate in the introductory portion. *Timeless Motion,* by Daniel Kobialka, is a spiritually uplifting version of Pachelbel's "Canon" that is an excellent background for this prayer/blessing/meditation.

Close your eyes and take a good stretch. . . . . . Become aware of your breathing. . . . . . Notice how your body rises gently on the inbreath and relaxes on the outbreath. . . . . . Every outbreath is an opportunity to let go and to become present to the flow. . . . . . Imagine that you can breathe in the divine Spirit as a radiant white light, coming in through the top of your head and swirling through your body as you breathe out. . . . . . Allow the light to flow through you and pour down upon you as if you were standing in a sunbeam. . . . . . Breathing in a sunbeam. . . . . . Surrounded by its radiance and warmth, which extends around you in a large circle.

See yourself at twenty or twenty-one years old, entering the circle of light. Look into the eyes of this young adult who is just learning to make her (his) way in the world and express her own uniqueness. Let her feel your support for all the joys and sorrows, trials and learnings that you know are in store for her. . . . . . See yourself at twelve or thirteen—on the brink of womanhood or manhood— entering the circle and holding hands with your young adult self. Look into the eyes of this young person who is just beginning to feel the stirring of the lifeforce as sexuality. What do you most wish that someone had told you about being a woman (or a man)? Look into the eyes of your changing self and say those words. . . . . . See yourself at seven years old, entering the circle of light and holding hands with your twelve-year-old. Enjoy the radiance and innocence of this beautiful little being who values intuition as much as intellect. . . . . . And now behold. A radiant angel enters the light and places your infant self into the arms of your seven-year-old. Look into those eyes, filled with ageless wisdom and newborn innocence. In full knowl-edge of all that beautiful infant has endured in its search for wisdom and freedom, give it your greatest respect and love. Now imagine that you could tuck all these children into your heart, and repeat the following blessings for your-self:

"May I be at peace. May I know the beauty of my own true nature. May my heart remain open. May I be healed."

Call to mind one or several friends or loved ones in as much detail as you can. . . . . . See them in the circle of light and focus on them with great respect and love. . . . . .

"May you be at peace. May you know the beauty of your own true nature. May your heart remain open. May you be healed."

Call to mind one or more people that you feel in conflict with. See them standing in the light. . . . . .

"May you be at peace. May you know the beauty of your own true nature. May your heart be open. May you be healed."

See our delicate planet, suspended like a jewel in the velvet blackness of space. Her white clouds, blue waters and green continents. . . . . . Imagine her fiery core, majestic mountains, plants and animals . . . . . . a living, breathing being of light.

"May there be peace on earth. May the hearts of all beings be open to one another. May all life reach its fullest poten-tial. May all life reflect the glory of the light."

Once again, feel yourself surrounded, enfolded and illu-minated by the circle of light. . . . . . If there is anything in your heart that you need to say to God, do so now. . . . . .

Dear One, Father/Mother of All, thank you for the gift of life.

Amen.

You can extend this meditation limitlessly, blessing the living and the dead, the saints and the sinners, the trouble spots in your neigh-borhood or anywhere on earth. You can also practice *metta* without reciting what my Jewish mother would have called in Yiddish the "whole megilla," the entire litany. If a friend comes to mind during the day, you might send loving-kindness to that one person. If an enemy or a person with whom you have a problem comes to mind, you can often shift your whole mood by blessing them instead of staying stuck in anger or feelings of victimization. If you are watching the news and start feeling hopeless about the condition of the world, you can offer a blessing and reorient to a higher vision that gives you courage, hope and ideas for taking practical action to bring about peace on earth.

CHAPTER ELEVEN
Peace and Healing

If a child smiles, if an adult smiles, that is very important. If in our daily life we can smile, if we can be peaceful and happy, not only we, but everyone will profit from it. This is the most basic kind of peace work.

Thich Nhat Hanh

Did you ever find yourself walking down the street on an early spring day, flowers coming up everywhere, the world fresh with the promise of new life and your mind full of income tax returns? Our worries show on our face, a fact that didn't escape a stranger as I was walking through the Boston Common on just such a day. "Hey," he yelled, to get my attention. "How about a smile? Life can't be all that bad." As I rearranged my features and turned up the corners of my mouth, a curious thing happened. I felt better. I started to become mindful of the stunning profusion of daffodils and crocuses that were a splendid counterpoint to the tender green of unfurling buds. I smelled the damp earth, felt the warm sun and noticed myself growing peaceful.

Thich Nhat Hanh is a Vietnamese Buddhist monk, poet and writer who brings a fresh perspective to peace of mind as a natural consequence of becoming mindful of the wonders of life all around us. Author of several books on meditation and mindfulness, he has worked tirelessly not only for personal but for global peace. Once nominated for the Nobel Peace Prize by Martin Luther King, Jr., he leads workshops and retreats internationally. A slight man who exudes joy, gratitude and humility, Thich Nhat Hanh has inspired millions of people with his down-to-earth, compassionate spirituality.

In listening to him, or in reading his books, one is reminded that every breath is an opportunity for living life mindfully rather than staying caught up in our worries and fears. In *A Guide to Walking Meditation,* he comments that every step we take leaves the imprint of our state—worry or joyfulness—on the earth as we pass:

> If I had the Buddha's eyes and could see through everything, I could discern the marks of worry and sorrow you leave in your footprints after you pass, like the scientist who can detect tiny living beings in a drop of pond water with a microscope. Walk so that your footprints bear only the marks of peaceful joy and complete freedom. To do this, you have to learn to let go—let go of your sorrows, let go of your worries. That is the secret of walking meditation.

WHAT, ME WORRY?

My mother was a first-class worrier who could imagine the worst tragedies and disasters with little or no evidence to support her awfulizing. If my brother, Alan, was ten minutes late for his curfew, in her mind he was either kidnapped or dead in an accident. If I got a pimple on my forehead she would worry about it invading the nerves and turning into a brain abcess. If my father made enough money to invest some in stocks, she would worry about the market crashing. If everyone was well, she would worry that someone might get sick. No matter what was happening in the present, she couldn't enjoy it because the "what ifs" kept her fearful of the future.

In addition to the "what ifs," a really world-class worrier spends plenty of time wallowing in misery with the "if onlys." If only I had married Jack my life would have been wonderful. If only my parents had been better I would have grown up to be happy and successful. If only I had saved more money I would feel secure right now. If only I had taken a right turn instead of a left that accident would never have happened. If only I had gone to college, or seen a doctor, or made different friends or moved to a different town or taken another job or listened to my mother. The regrets and resentments that "if onlys" represent are a major source of unhappiness that can keep us stuck for a lifetime.

It is amazing that many people who are actually in the throes of crisis—coping with divorce, illness, financial disaster or grief—are often no more unhappy than people in ordinary circumstances who are literally worrying themselves to death about nothing. Have you ever sat in your living room, safe and warm, while your mind spun disaster? Have you ever lain awake at night rerunning conversations, worrying about finances, nursing grievances or obsessing about your own or somebody else's health? Has it ever helped?

Some people do think that worrying is helpful because they mistake it for planning. But worry is distinctly different from planning. Planning has a purpose and a goal, is informed by creativity, leads to constructive change and increases energy. Worry has no constructive purpose, is informed by fear and leads to confusion and exhaustion. When you catch yourself worrying, think about how you could shift gears by switching into constructive planning or by letting go of what isn't happening through tuning into what is.

It takes practice to give up worrying, and one of the ways we can learn to do that is by practicing mindful attention in all our activities. Dr. Jon Kabat-Zinn's book *Full Catastrophe Living* is an excellent primer on mindfulness. Based on the Stress Reduction and Relaxation Program that he founded and directs at the University of Massachusetts Medical School, the book presents an in-depth program for letting go of stress, pain and worries by becoming mindful of the wonders of life all around us. This means really paying attention to taste and texture when we eat; listening to people when they talk, thinking carefully when we plan, and sensing the world around us with joy and gratitude when we walk.

INSTRUCTIONS FOR WALKING MEDITATION

Mindful walking is an excellent way to start developing increased awareness in all of our activities. When you are caught up in worries, you are effectively absent from your body. There's nobody home. You may be walking down a beautiful street, for example, but you don't see the scenery. Instead, you focus on inner scenes of preoccupation, worry or fear. By shifting your attention to the present moment—to the bodily sensations of breathing and walking and to the nuances of the scenery around you—you come back into your body and into control of your mind. A simple act like walking then becomes a meditation, an opening to the divine presence.

Mindful walking is an effective meditation practice in its own right, or it can be combined with sitting meditation or prayer. Anytime you are out walking, try letting go of your cares by becoming mindful of what is. Your efforts to be mindful will not only make walking more enjoyable for the moment but also strengthen your mental muscles for letting go in all situations. Little by little, you will become more peaceful. The following instructions for mindful walking are adapted from Thich Nhat Hanh's *A Guide to Walking Meditation*.

• Find a beautiful setting to walk in if you can, but any place will do. Even a small room will suffice.
• Notice, as Thich Nhat Hanh says, that *this world contains all the wonders you could expect to find in heaven itself*. Open your awareness to the colors, the fragrances of earth and sky or the details of whatever setting you are in.
• Become aware of your body as you walk. Notice the pleasant rhythm of your breathing. *Walk slowly and concentrate on each step*. Be aware of each movement—lifting the foot, shifting your weight, placing the foot back down. Can you walk in rhythm with your breath?
• Walk with dignity, humility and self-respect. Think of a being who embodies these qualities. Walk like the Buddha, Mother Teresa or Jesus—or like your Aunt Sue if she calls these qualities to mind for you!

• Ask yourself why you carry around such a heavy load of worry and sorrow. *Let compassion well up in your heart as you feel the pain that worry and sorrow cause you. From this compassionate awareness decide to stop worrying and let go of your sorrow.* Thich Nhat Hanh advises, "If you want to you can—like taking off a raincoat and shaking off all the raindrops that are clinging to it."

• Bring a little smile to your face. Thich Nhat Hanh suggests the following meditative poem:

> Breathing in I calm body and mind (inbreath)
> Breathing out I smile (outbreath)
> Dwelling in the present moment (inbreath)
> I know this is the only moment (outbreath)

• Try walking to the rhythm of the poem and the breath. It will keep you light and remind you that every moment is an opportunity to be born anew and to see the miracles of everyday existence with the freshness of a child, with what Rabbi Abraham Heschel calls *radical amazement*.

Thich Nhat Hanh ends *A Guide to Walking Meditation* by speaking of the universal compassion that mindful awareness of life creates:

> The practice of walking meditation opens your eyes to wonders in the universe. It turns samsara (the world of illusions) into Pure Land (heaven). It lets sorrow and worry fall away, and brings peace. But walking meditation also helps us to see pain, anguish and suffering. When we are aware we can see clearly what is happening in life. . . . Scented paths across the the rice fields, shady bamboo-lined dirt roads, parks covered with dark-colored dry leaves— these are your paths for walking meditation; please enjoy them. They should not lead you to forgetfulness, but should bring you the necessary mindfulness so that you can see the real dramas of the world. Then every path, every street—from the back alleys of Beirut to the roads of Vietnam where mines still explode and take the lives of children and farmers—every path in the world is your walking medi-

tation path. Once you are awake, you will not hesitate to enter these paths. . . . You will suffer, but your pain will not come from your own worries and fears. You will suffer because of your kinship with all beings, because you have the compassion of an awakened being, a Bodhisattva.

COMPASSIONATE ACTION

Compassion, like charity, begins at home. The first step toward deep healing is self-healing. Only after we have remembered to respect and care for ourselves can we truly enter into "kinship with all beings." If we try to help others before we have healed our wounds and developed compassion for ourselves, we may find that the basis of our rescuing and helping of others is codependency rather than co-creation.

I enjoy reading about the lives of people who are models for compassionate action. Peace Pilgrim was a humble, silver-haired woman who walked penniless across the country seven times—more than 25,000 miles—for peace between 1953 and her death in 1981. Vowing to remain a wanderer until humankind learned the ways of peace, she crisscrossed the country carrying her only possessions, a comb and a toothbrush, in the pocket of her blue smock. She ate when and if she was given food and slept wherever there was shelter, many times alongside the road.

The way to world peace, according to Peace Pilgrim, is through attaining inner peace and then putting what you learn into compassionate action. When asked where she learned meditation, Peace Pilgrim answered, "I did not learn meditation. I just walked, receptive and silent, amid the beauty of nature—and put the wonderful insights that came to me into practice." Her pilgrimage and philosophy are summarized in the book *Peace Pilgrim: Her Life and Work in Her Own Words*, compiled by friends after her death from her letters, interviews in the media and tapes of her many lectures.

Her philosophy puts spirituality to a practical test by offering us the challenge that *If we truly believe in the divine power of love, we must live by it*. Peace Pilgrim says:

I once said to a woman who believed in war and Christian values: "On the one hand you talk about Christian values, on the other hand you say, 'Isn't force the only deterrent they respect?' This has been our trouble down through the ages—we have given only lip service to Christian values, and lived by the jungle law of tooth and claw. We have quoted *'Be not overcome of evil, overcome evil with good'* and then attempted to overcome evil with more evil. We worship God, but have no faith in the working of God's law of love. The world awaits the living of the law of love, which will reach the divine within all human beings and transform them"(p. 103).

Since I was reading Peace Pilgrim during the war in the Persian Gulf in the winter of 1990/1991, her thoughts on war were particularly relevant. What would happen if nations really did live the law of love? We can watch what happens in the years to come by observing the progress of the Tibetan Buddhists who embody the ideals of nonviolence. In the 1950s, when one of the worst holocausts of all time was committed in Tibet by the Chinese, millions of Tibetans were slaughtered, some were captured and tortured, and most of the remainder were driven from their homeland into exile in India.

The pristine, virgin land of Tibet was raped and mutilated. The mountains were blasted and mined for minerals. Huge herds of wildlife were decimated. Six thousand monasteries were torched, and Tibet was reduced to a wasteland. Remarkably, the rest of the world heard little about the holocaust. The Tibetans relocated in India under the direction of the Dalai Lama, the secular and spiritual head of the Tibetan people. For this group there is no division between church and state—they are one. Their secular policy rests firmly on their spiritual beliefs of harmlessness toward all living creatures, even one's enemies.

In 1989 Myrin and I attended the First International Conference on Holistic Health and Medicine in Bangalore, India, which was cosponsored by His Holiness the Dalai Lama. While traveling through southern India we had the opportunity to visit a Tibetan resettlement camp. The land around the camp was poor and arid. Poverty was endemic to the area, yet the camp bloomed with activity and relative prosperity. Working together, the Tibetans had developed agriculture suitable for the region and were raising abundant, healthy crops. They had built a school, a monastery, a temple and adequate housing for all the refugees. The weaving of Tibetan rugs and the carving of magnificent wooden items provided the community with goods for export. The prosperity and industry of the Tibetans, furthermore, was helping the Indian citizens who lived in the surrounding area.

Myrin and I had driven unknown and unannounced into the camp, yet we were treated with the greatest respect and kindness. Two monks who spoke English discovered us, offered us tea and showed us around. When we expressed sorrow over the plight of the Tibetan people, the monks agreed that the exodus had been difficult and expressed the hope that someday they would be able to return peacefully to their homeland, a land in which the Dalai Lama hopes to create sanctuary for animals and people who are in need. At no time was a harsh word uttered about the Chinese. Instead, the monks' whole demeanor was reminiscent of Jesus' on the cross when he blessed his murderers, saying, "Forgive them, Father, for they know not what they do."

In the course of studying meditation I have met the Dalai Lama and several Tibetan Buddhist monks. They all have the same forgiving attitude toward the Chinese. They bless them, acknowledging that the perpetration of evil can only come from ignorance. They also accept the Tibetan holocaust as part of some larger divine plan that is working according to its own schedule. In Western society we are socialized to hate injustice and to fight back, so at first it may seem quite a stretch to understand the Tibetan Buddhist point of view. But leaving our beliefs aside, what fruits has the philosophy of forgiveness borne for the exiled Tibetans?

In 1989 the Dalai Lama received the Nobel Peace Prize, bringing the plight of the Tibetans to worldwide attention and engendering a real curiosity about the spiritual life of Tibet. The Tibetan refugees have used their energy to rebuild their lives—preserving their spirituality and culture—rather than spending it in hatred for the Chinese. Vengefulness binds one firmly to the object of hate. The forgiveness of the Tibetans, in contrast, gives them freedom, even in exile.

During the Nazi holocaust there were also people who managed to maintain compassion and freedom during a living hell. One of those was the young Dutch Jew Etty Hillesum. After she perished in Auschwitz in her late twenties, her diaries were found and published as *An Interrupted Life: The Diaries of Etty Hillesum 1941–1943*. On September 23, 1943, she wrote in a letter to her friend Klaas:

> All I really wanted to say is this; we have so much work to do on ourselves that we shouldn't even be thinking of hating our so-called enemies. We are hurtful enough to one another as it is. . . . and I repeat with the same old passion, although I am gradually beginning to think that I am being tiresome, "It is the only thing we can do, Klaas, I see no alternative, each of us must turn inwards and destroy in himself all that he thinks he ought to destroy in others. And remember that every atom of hate we add to this world makes it still more inhospitable" (p. 222).

As Pogo said so long ago, "We have met the enemy and he is us." Until each one of us, individually and as a collective culture, heals the wounds of our past and forgives our enemies we will continue to dehumanize one another and hurt others as we ourselves have been hurt. The key to deep healing and the attainment of inner peace is forgiveness. There can never be peace on earth until there is peace within our own souls.

CONVERTING SUFFERING TO SERVICE

Our world is full of people whose compassion has awakened through confronting difficulty and darkness, worry and sorrow. I was working on this chapter when a film crew arrived to interview me for a documentary that will help people with cancer get the information they need about healing on the physical, mind/body and spiritual levels. The producer of the documentary was motivated to create the film because his wife died from cancer and such a film would have been of real help to them as they sought safe passage through the new and frightening territory of life with cancer.

In a similar way, Leslie Kussman, a friend of mine who had never made a film in her life, produced an award-winning documentary on grieving for children. When her mother died, Leslie had a five-year-old daughter and was pregnant with her second child. She didn't know how to help her daughter grieve, and as part of her own grieving she spoke with other families in similar circumstances. Many of them, along with experts like psychiatrist Elisabeth Kübler-Ross, M.D., shared their wisdom and experiences in Leslie's wonderfully healing videotape.

Tricia Stallman, a friend of both Leslie's and mine, likewise converted suffering into service. Tricia was diagnosed with ovarian cancer in the mid-1980s. Following multiple surgeries and several rounds of chemotherapy, Tricia lived well for six and a half years before she died with dignity and peace in October 1991. Trained as a social worker, she founded a support community called Hope for cancer patients and their families in Providence, Rhode Island. Hope is staffed with both professionals and volunteers who were inspired by Tricia's love, laughter and the courage to live each day fully in spite of recurrent cancer.

Alcoholism and drug addiction are other areas in which personal suffering and subsequent recovery often lead to service. The final step in twelve-step recovery programs, in fact, specifically states the intent to help others achieve sobriety as part of the addict's ongoing process of healing and growth in self-awareness. Sometimes, though, when we look around this world there is so much suffering that we don't know where to start. Unlike Leslie or Tricia or a recovering alcoholic, we may not have suffered and learned from a specific difficulty, from where we can pass our experience on to another person.

When our world is so obviously full of famine, war, disease, political oppression, prejudice, poverty and hatred, where can a single person begin to make a difference? Sometimes the world's problems seem so overwhelming that we feel paralyzed. In *Words to Love By,* Mother Teresa offers a simple solution, the idea of starting by helping just one person—as she says, the secret of one, one, one:

I never look at the masses as my responsibility. I look at the individual. I can love only one person at a time. I can feed only one person at a time. Just one, one, one. . . . So you begin. . . . I begin. I picked up one person—maybe if I didn't pick up that one person I wouldn't have picked up 42,000. The whole work is only a drop in the ocean. But if I didn't put the drop in, the ocean would be one drop less. Same thing for you, same thing in your family, same thing in the church where you go. Just begin . . . one, one, one (p. 79).

We can start to alleviate suffering by looking into the eyes of a family member or friend and telling them something kind and encouraging. And when we come together to do this in groups, life becomes altogether a more joyful, peaceful enterprise.

CREATING HEALING COMMUNITIES

Until the spring of 1988 I commuted the infamous Southeast Expressway, better known as the Distressway, for at least an hour each way to work at one of Boston's Harvard Medical Area teaching hospitals. Adding two hours of commuting to a full day of work left little time for socializing in my home town, and after living there for five years Myrin and I knew very few people. When I left hospital practice and academia to work at home, I discovered that all my friends lived in suburbs closer to Boston and that I still had to commute to see them.

The situation changed dramatically when a woman Myrin and I had met at Sunday services at a local, ecumenical spiritual center decided to have a small gathering of women at her home to celebrate the winter solstice in late December 1989. Chanukah, Christmas, winter solstice and New Year have strong commonalities. They come at the darkest time of the year and mark the re-entrance of the light.

Winter solstice itself is the darkest day of the year, the turning point after which the days begin to lengthen. Our little group of solstice celebrators lighted a fire to symbolize the return of the light, and each of us lit an individual candle as well. We meditated and looked within for an old belief or habit that was blocking the return of the light in our own life, wrote it on a piece of paper and then shared it with the group. That done, we fed our papers to the fire, affirming our individual and collective prayer to let go of these old patterns. We drank hot cider, ate some goodies, sang together and began the process of bonding through sharing a little of our life stories.

The friendships that began that evening ripened into a woman's group that remained together for a year and a half before it opened to the larger community as a quarterly healing circle that meets on the Sunday afternoon nearest to each solstice and equinox. Twenty-five to fifty people generally come through word of mouth. The healing circles incorporate joyful (and sometimes downright raucous) singing, meditation and prayer. In addition, any person who wants special support comes into the center of the circle and asks for what they need. People who feel particularly close to them, or who have been through similar difficulties in their own life, gather around and give their help.

It is difficult to describe the sense of connectedness, caring and compassion that happens in these circles without sounding flaky, strange or trite—but I'll try anyway! At one circle, for example, a woman whose breast cancer had just recurred came into the center. Two women who had also lived with cancer joined her, held her hands, validated her feelings and shared some of their own healing stories. Three other women affirmed her strength and offered continuing support. We then did a short healing light meditation and sang her a song. There was a lot of joy, a few tears and a wonderful feeling of closeness and community. The rest of the large group supported the process with their attention and by participating in the meditation and singing.

Deep bonds grow in these healing circles, leading to lasting friendships. Regardless of a person's age, sex or belief system, the healing circle is a form of loving support that is always spontaneous, fresh and exciting. One never knows what to expect, how people will come together and what kind of healing will emerge from the evening. The point of the circles is not to promote physical healing, but to provide support, build community and promote a deeper spiritual healing, of which physical healing may sometimes be a part. Prayers are ecumenical and offered in the spirit "May the best potential in this person or situation be realized." We like to leave the outcome to an Intelligence greater than our own.

In addition to attending the meditation and healing circles, my husband, Myrin, has been a member of a men's group for several years. Their group of five began by each man taking two evenings to share his life story with the other group members. They then spent several sessions writing and sharing their spiritual autobiographies, a process developed by Reverend Carl Scoville at the King's Chapel in Boston, that has been popularized by writer Dan Wakefield. His fine book, *The Story of Your Life: Writing Your Spiritual Autobiography,* describes a group process that leads to personal revelation and a deep bonding with the other participants.

Although I've never attended one of their meetings, I have been in the house at the time, and I can report that the men spend half an hour or more drumming together. Drumming is currently undergoing a major cultural renaissance. Robert Bly, whose best-selling book *Iron John* helped launch the men's movement, holds workshops across the country. Myrin and our son Justin attended one of these weekend workshops with two other friends and were delighted with the storytelling, drumming and community they shared with 600 other men. They were also empowered by men giving men permission to cry and do the grieving that is the first step toward deep healing.

Women, unlike men, are culturally and constitutionally comfortable with intimacy, yet we too are searching for new models of community. The women's movement, once informed solely by the need for political and economic equality, is being enlarged by adding the search for deep healing and new forms of spirituality. Riane Eisler's powerful book *The Chalice and the Blade* is a fascinating account of the transition from the "old religion" in which the Goddess was worshipped to male-centered religions in which a "thundergod" became preeminent. This shift, which occurred about 5,000 or 6,000 years ago, coincided with the advent of Judaism and was carried forward by Christianity. During the shift from Goddess to God, what

Eisler calls "partnership" societies in which men and women cooper-
ated were replaced by "dominator" societies in which men placed
themselves above women.

I believe that we are now at a new crossroads, both politically and
spiritually, where males and females are once again beginning to work
in partnership. The emerging men's movement and the enlarging
women's movement are evidence of this shift. Both groups are looking for a new way to define themselves personally—in intimate relationship, as parents, in work, in community and as spiritual beings—
a way that will bring deep healing to the larger community.

This last decade of the twentieth century promises to be a time
during which we will reestablish connectedness with ourselves, with
one another, with other nations, with the earth, with the sacred.
Wherever you are, you can begin the process of planetary healing by
participating in your own healing. And you can quicken your own
healing by joining with like-minded others. Why not form a support
group, a meditation group, a men's or women's group or a healing
circle where you are. Even two people are enough to start. In this
way, as Mother Teresa would say, one by one by one we can help
achieve world peace by working toward inner peace.

CHAPTER TWELVE

Practicalities of Soul Making— Ten Survival Tips

The present is the point where time touches eternity.

Archimandrite Kallistos Ware

A friend of mine who read an early manuscript of this book handed it back with succinct advice. "The philosophy is great, but unless you remind people of the most basic things like proper breathing, stretching, diet, sleep and support they are apt to get so stressed out when the going gets tough that they'll forget all the philosophy." And Celia was right. When we are going through a dark night, we are likely to throw caution and balance to the winds. We may drink more coffee or alcohol, eat poorly, lose sleep and let go of the very practices—like meditation, walking, exercise or prayer—that we most need. So here are ten practical tips that will help you survive the dark night and emerge strong at the coming of the dawn.

1. Make a point of paying close attention to your physical needs, as indicated below. Proper breathing, exercise, eating and sleeping habits often go down the drain during hard times, adding physical stress to mental stress and creating a vicious cycle.

• *Breathing.* If your breath is fast and shallow, you are creating stress, anxiety and panic. You can relax quickly by switching to diaphragmatic breathing. Take in a long, deep breath through your mouth and blow it out slowly and completely. Allow the next breath to come in through your nose, and imagine that it is inflating your belly like a balloon. When you exhale, imagine your belly deflating. Take ten or more of these relaxing breaths frequently throughout the day.

• *Take stretch breaks.* Several times a day close your eyes and mentally scan your body for tension. Stretch out tight spots before they become pain spots. You can find instructions for simple stretching exercises that can be done at your desk, on an airplane or any place at all in *Minding the Body, Mending the Mind.* In addition to stretching, give your body a daily workout with exercise you enjoy. Mindful walking is a great way to rest both body and mind.

• *Eat well.* In general the more stressed people get, the worse their diet becomes because of the tendency to go for quick fixes of sugar and fat that destroy the appetite for better fare. Eat lots of whole grains, vegetables and fruits at regular mealtimes. Eliminate or minimize caffeine and alcohol, and drink plenty of water to help your body flush out toxins.

• *Stick to a reasonable sleep schedule.* If your troubles insist on running through your mind like hamsters on a wheel, sit up in bed and meditate. If you fall asleep meditating, fine. If you don't, you still will have gotten some mental and physical rest. Avoid relying on the radio or TV as sleep aids since your unconscious mind is a sponge for empty chatter, violence and the stress of those nasty, loud ads. Try playing music instead. Cassette players with headphones let you listen without disturbing others. The Resources section of this book lists several tapes that are particularly relaxing.

2. Saint John of the Cross taught that interior silence is the place where Spirit secretly anoints the soul and heals our deepest wounds. Make time during the day to be alone—not to read or watch TV—but to be quiet. Garden, sit outside, walk mindfully, go into nature, meditate, be with music. Most of us will give our time and energy away to others, leaving little for ourselves. The disbalance that occurs when you squeeze yourself out of your own life creates new stress

that prevents the healing of old pain. Save time to let silence be a partner in your healing.

3. Find the support you need. Whether it is a grief group, an illness support group, a twelve-step program, an incest survivor's program, an individual or group therapy situation, *make sure that you feel supported in growing and changing, not in staying sick, victimized or dependent.* Identifying yourself as a victim is fine in the first steps of healing when you are grieving your losses and expressing your anger. But deep healing requires you to let go of being a victim and to move on and pick up your power.

4. Put the serenity prayer into action:

God grant me the serenity to accept the things I cannot change,
The courage to change the things I can and
The wisdom to know the difference.

There is no use worrying over what you cannot change. It is a point-less exercise in fear. Be realistic about your situation and take action where you can. To be serene about what can't be changed, and to have the wisdom to know the difference, requires repairing to the cave of your heart. There, in your center, you will know what to do. But you have to know how to find your center. This is the value of taking time to be silent and learning to empty your mind of chatter through meditation or mindfulness.

5. Anthropologist Angeles Arrien wrote down these four rules for living. They are worth reflecting on:

• Show up.
• Pay attention.
• Tell the truth.
• Don't be attached to the results.

My husband tells me that I am pretty good about the first three rules; it's with the fourth that I still need a lot of practice! We often create suffering by being attached to the results of what we do even though we did the best we could. Remember the first line of the medieval poet Wolfram's grail poem: "Every action has both good and evil results. The best we can do is to intend the good."

6. Remind yourself that it is good to be alive! Try this exercise. When you get ready to brush your teeth in the morning, stand in front of the mirror and close your eyes. Remember a holy moment and focus on the feelings of peace, interconnectedness, energy, vitality and safety that it brings to body and mind. *Feel* what it is to be alive. Then look at yourself in the mirror[1] and say, "Good morning, how are you?" Feel your aliveness and respond, "I am alive and I am grateful and today—for the benefit of myself, my family and all beings—I will (add an affirmation here)." It is helpful to repeat the affirmation aloud two or three times.

7. Practice loving-kindness. Begin with respect and love for yourself, affirming these or other good wishes.

> *May I be at peace.*
> *May my heart remain open.*
> *May I know the beauty of my own true nature.*
> *May I be healed.*

Then send these loving-kindness thoughts to others.

8. Remember that you have the right to be happy. The best outcome of crisis is a return to our own true nature, to the inmost center or Higher Self. The attributes of that peaceful core are not only wisdom and compassion but also joy and happiness. But even if happiness hasn't yet sprung up naturally as part of your healing, you can get a sneak preview by remembering to smile. Shakespeare said, "Practice a virtue if you have it not."

---

[1] This part of the exercise is based on a recommendation of the Native American teacher Dhyani Ywahoo, in her book *Voices of Our Ancestors.*

9. Once upon a time a poor old man chastised God for failing to answer his prayers to win the lottery. God shook her head and replied, "For heaven's sake, Sam, at least you could have bought a ticket!" Seen and unseen helpers *will respond* when you ask for help. But there are some guidelines for getting it. First, you have to ask. Second, you need to do your share to bring about positive changes.

10. If you don't seem to be getting what you asked for, despite doing your part to make it happen, perhaps you are getting what you need. Maybe winning the lottery, as delightful as it might have seemed, would actually have impeded Sam's soul growth. Maybe a rapid end to your troubles would deprive you of a deep healing that is in your best interest. A wise prayer in crisis is not for crisis to end, but for the strength and courage to endure the passage. Indian poet/saint Rabindranath Tagore said,

> *Let me not pray to be sheltered from dangers*
> *   but to be fearless in facing them.*
> *Let me not beg for the stilling of my pain but*
> *   for the heart to conquer it.*
> *Let me not crave in anxious fear to be saved*
> *   but hope for the patience to win my*
> *   freedom.*

CHAPTER THIRTEEN
Night Lights

The breeze at dawn has secrets to tell you.
> *Don't go back to sleep.*
You must ask for what you really want.
> *Don't go back to sleep.*
People are going back and forth across the doorsill
> *where the two worlds touch.*
The door is round and open.
> *Don't go back to sleep.*

Rumi

But we do go back to sleep. For a while we peer through the doorway between the worlds and see the light behind the shadows. Then the doorway seems to close and we fall back into our ruminations. Was the love and peace we felt a dream? Or is suffering itself a dream? The nature of life is flow and change. We wake up for a while and remember the soul stories that urge us on to freedom. Then we fall asleep again and forget. This chapter consists of little stories, prayers and quotes—touchstones of light—that can help us stay awake.

I learned a lot about touchstones from my friend Lee, who is a person with AIDS. We were having lunch together one bright spring day in New York City, talking about how difficult it can be to keep the faith and how objects that evoke loving memories can help. I showed Lee my little leather "medicine bag" full of sacred items—a silver dollar my father had given me as a child, a rose petal that had been on Mom's pillow when she died, a crystal that was given to me by a friend, a jade snake that reminds me of overcoming old fears and a piece of a white silk scarf that the Dalai Lama had given me as part of a traditional Buddhist greeting.

Lee reached into his pocket and pulled out a strand of "pop-it" beads, the kind that you may have played with when you were a child. Each bead represented a friend to him and held a memory of a special time with that person. To me it was like a rosary of the heart, a remembrance of everything most precious in a lifetime. Several weeks later I received a package in the mail from Lee containing a glass flagon suspended from a leather thong. Inside was lavender oil distilled by the monks at a twelfth-century abbey in Senanque, France. It was on a visit there, in the lavender fields, that he had put the bead of our friendship on his strand. Whenever I smell the oil, or see the flagon, I am sustained by the love it brings to mind.

The quotes, prayers and poems in this chapter are like such a strand of touchstones for me and I hope that they will be a comfort and a reminder of divine love for you.

> *A monk was once asked, what do you do there*
> *in the monastery?*
> *He replied, "We fall and get up, fall and get up,*
> *fall and get up again."*

> **Tito Colliander**

A soul is forged out of fire and rock crystal.
Something rigorous, hard in an
Old Testament sense, but also as gentle
as the gesture with which his tender
fingertips sometimes stroked my eyelashes.

> Etty Hillesum,
> from a concentration camp

> Only by contact with evil
> could I have learned to feel
> by contrast the beauty of
> truth and love and goodness.

> Helen Keller

When there is no longer a cyclone, there is no
longer an eye. So the storms, crises and suffer-
ings of life are a way of finding the eye. When
everything is going our way we do not see the
eye and feel no need to look for it. But when
everything is going against us, then we find
the eye.

> Bernadette Roberts

To one who waits
all things reveal themselves,
so long as you have the courage
not to deny in the darkness
what you have seen in the light.

Coventry Patmore

I have lived on the lip
of insanity, wanting to know reasons,
knocking on a door. It opens.
I've been knocking from the inside!

Rumi

Ask and it shall be given you.
Seek, and ye shall find.
Knock, and it shall be opened to you.

Jesus, in Matthew 7:7

While troubles will come, they are
   always temporary—nothing lasts
forever. Thus, there is the famous
legend that King Solomon, the wisest
man of all times, had a ring inscribed
with the words, "This too will pass."

                  Rabbi Aryeh Kaplan

And God said . . . I do set my bow in the cloud,

      and it shall be for a token of a covenant
      between me and the earth. And it shall come
      to pass, when I bring a cloud over the earth,
      that the (rain)bow shall be seen in the cloud.

                  The Book of Genesis

            See!
            I will not
            forget you . . .

            I have carved
            you
            on the palm
            of my hand.

                  Isaiah 49:15

The pain was great when the strings
were being tuned, my Master!
Begin your music, and let me forget the
pain, let me feel in beauty what you had
in your mind through those pitiless days.

Rabindranath Tagore

Lord, since Thou hast taken from me
all that I had of Thee, yet of Thy grace
leave me the gift which every dog has
by nature: that of being true to Thee
in my distress, when I am deprived
of all consolation. This I desire more
fervently than Thy heavenly Kingdom.
Amen.

Mechthild of Magdeberg

Remember this:
Be still and know that I am God.
Don't ever forget who you are!
You cannot be where God is not.

Peace Pilgrim

The Lord is my shepherd
I shall not want.
He maketh me to lie down in green pastures.
He leadeth me beside the still waters.
He restoreth my soul.
He leadeth me in paths of righteousness
For his name's sake.

Yea, though I walk through the valley
Of the Shadow of Death I fear no evil
For Thou art with me,
Thy rod and thy staff they comfort me.

Thou preparest a table before me
In the presence of mine enemies.
Thou anointest my head with oil.
My cup runneth over.
Surely goodness and mercy shall
follow me all the days of my life
And I will dwell in the house of the Lord
Forever.

Psalm 23

The Lord is my light and my salvation.
Whom shall I fear?
The Lord is the stronghold of my life;
of whom shall I be afraid?

From Psalm 27

Whither shall I go from thy Spirit?
Or whither shall I flee from thy presence?

If I ascend to heaven, thou art there!
If I make my bed in hell, thou art there!

If I take the wings of the morning
and dwell in the uttermost parts of the sea
even there thy hand shall lead me
and thy right hand shall hold me.

From Psalm 139

The Light of God surrounds us
The Love of God enfolds us
The Power of God protects us
The Presence of God watches over us.
Wherever we are, God is
And all is well.

Unity Church

If you are faced with a challenge,
refuse to be panic-stricken.
Life has not ended for you.
Life flows on. Declare for yourself:
I accept the reality of this situation,
but not its permanence.

Eric Butterworth

There is but one freedom,
to put oneself right with death.
After that everything is possible.
I cannot force you to believe in God.
Believing in God amounts to coming
to terms with death. When you have
accepted death, the problem of God
will be solved—and not the reverse.

                    Albert Camus

                    Birth and death
                    are not two different states,
                    but they are different aspects
                    of the same state.

                            Gandhi

                    From the unreal lead us to the Real,
                    From darkness lead us to Light.
                    From death lead us to immortality.

                            The Upanishads

When we come to the last moment
of this lifetime, and we look back across it,
the only thing that's going to matter is
"What was the quality of our love?"

                    Richard Bach

One of the reasons why people
give up hope is that they look at
their own contemporaries and
imagine them to be far worthier
than they themselves are.

       Rabbi Nachman

A whole person is one who
has both walked with God
and wrestled with the devil.

       C. G. Jung

Out beyond ideas of
wrongdoing and rightdoing,
there is a field.
I'll meet you there.

       Rumi

Our first duty is
not to hate ourselves.

       Swami Vivekananda

God regards with merciful eyes
not what you are nor what you
have been but what you wish to be.

The Cloud of Unknowing

When I have forgiven myself
and remembered who I am,
I will bless everyone and
everything I see.

A Course in Miracles

On centering prayer:

It is as if God planted a great big kiss in
the middle of our spirit and all the
wounds, doubts, and guilt feelings were
all healed at the same moment.
The experience of being loved by the
Ultimate Mystery banishes every fear.
It convinces us that all the mistakes we
have made and all the sins we have
committed are completely forgiven and
forgotten.

Father Thomas Keating

Every good thing you do,
every good thing you say,
every good thought you think,
vibrates on and on and never
ceases. The evil remains only
until it is overcome by the good,
but the good remains forever.

> **Peace Pilgrim**

The holiest of all the spots on earth
is where an ancient hatred has become
a present love.

> *A Course in Miracles*

The conclusion is always the same:
love is the most powerful and still the most
unknown energy of the world.

> **Pierre Teilhard de Chardin**

Let nothing disturb thee;
Let nothing dismay thee;
All things pass:
God never changes.
Patience attains
All that it strives for.
He who has God
Finds he lacks nothing:
God alone suffices.

Teresa of Avila

But all shall be well,
and all shall be well,
and all manner of thing
shall be well.

Julian of Norwich

God says: Ever you are
before my eyes.
God, I am your opus.
Before the beginning of time,
already then,
I was in your mind.

Hildegard of Bingen

Lord make me an instrument of thy peace.
 Where there is hatred, let me sow love.
 Where there is injury, pardon.
 Where there is doubt, faith.
 Where there is despair, hope.
 Where there is darkness, light.
 And where there is sadness, joy.

O, Divine Master, grant that I may not
 so much seek to be consoled as to console;
 to be understood, as to understand;
 to be loved, as to love;
 for it is in giving that we receive,
 it is in pardoning that we are pardoned,
 and it is in dying that we are born to eternal life.

Francis of Assisi

There are only two ways to live your life.
 One is as though nothing is a miracle.
 The other is as though everything is a miracle.

Albert Einstein

RESOURCES

BOOKS

Psychology

The Adventure of Self-Discovery. Stanislav Grof. State University of New York Press, New York, 1988.

Forgiveness: A Bold Choice for a Peaceful Heart. Robin Casarjian. Bantam Books, New York, 1992.

Full Catastrophe Living: Using the Wisdom of Your Body and Mind to Face Stress, Pain and Illness. Jon Kabat-Zinn, Ph.D. Delacorte Press, New York, 1990.

Guilt Is the Teacher, Love Is the Lesson. Joan Borysenko. Warner Books, New York, 1990.

Healing into Life and Death. Stephen Levine. Anchor Press/Doubleday, New York, 1987.

Healing the Shame That Binds You. John Bradshaw. Health Communications, Inc., Deerfield Beach, Florida, 1988.

Homecoming: Reclaiming and Championing Your Inner Child. John Bradshaw. Bantam Books, New York, 1990.

Learned Optimism. Martin E. P. Seligman, Ph.D. Knopf, New York, 1990.

A Little Book on the Human Shadow. Robert Bly. Harper & Row, San Francisco, 1988.

Love, Medicine and Miracles. Bernie Siegel, M. D. Harper & Row, San Francisco, 1987.

Man and His Symbols. Carl G. Jung. Doubleday, New York, 1964.

Man's Search for Meaning. Viktor E. Frankl. Washington Square Press, New York, 1959.

Meaning and Medicine: A Doctor's Stories of Breakthrough and Healing. Larry Dossey, M. D. Bantam Books, New York, 1991.

Minding the Body, Mending the Mind. Joan Borysenko. Bantam Books, New York, 1988.

Open Mind, Discriminating Mind: Reflections on Human Possibilities. Charles Tart. Harper & Row, San Francisco, 1989.

Peace, Love and Healing. Bernie Siegel, M. D. Harper & Row, San Francisco, 1989.

The Portable Jung. Edited by Joseph Campbell. Penguin Books, New York, 1971.

The Power of Myth. Joseph Campbell with Bill Moyers. Doubleday, New York, 1988.

Reach for the Rainbow: Advanced Healing for Survivors of Sexual Abuse. Lynne D. Finney, J. D., M.S.W. Perigee, New York, 1992.

The Revolution of Hope. Erich Fromm. Harper & Row, New York, 1968.

Shivitti: A Vision. Ka-Tzetnik 135633. Harper & Row, San Francisco, 1987.

Spiritual Emergency: When Personal Transformation Becomes a Crisis. Edited by Stanislav Grof, M. D., and Christina Grof. Jeremy Tarcher, Los Angeles, 1990.

Stages of Faith: The Psychology of Human Development and the Quest for Meaning. James W. Fowler. Harper & Row, New York, 1981.

The Stormy Search for the Self. Christina and Stanislav Grof, M.D. Jeremy Tarcher, Los Angeles, 1990.

Toward a Psychology of Being. Abraham H. Maslow. Van Nostrand Reinhold, New York, 1968.

The Light—Near-Death Experiences and Lucid Dreaming

Closer to the Light. Melvin Morse, M.D., with Paul Perry. Villard Books, New York, 1990.

Exploring the World of Lucid Dreaming. Stephen La Berge, Ph.D., and Howard Rheingold. Ballantine Books, New York, 1990.

Heading Toward Omega: In Search of the Meaning of the Near-Death Experience. Kenneth Ring. William Morrow, New York, 1985.

The Light Beyond. Raymond A. Moody, M.D., with Paul Perry. Bantam Books, New York, 1988.

Lucid Dreaming: Dawning of the Clear Light. G. Scott Sparrow. A.R.E. Press, Virginia Beach, Virginia, 1976.

The Sun and the Shadow: My Experiment with Lucid Dreaming. Kenneth Kelzer. A.R.E. Press, Virginia Beach, Virginia, 1987. An amazing book.

Exploring Past Lives

Born Again and Again. John Van Auken. Inner Vision, Virginia Beach, Virginia, 1989.

Coming Back: A Psychiatrist Explores Past Life Journeys. Raymond A. Moody, M.D., with Paul Perry. Bantam Books, New York, 1991.

Edgar Cayce: You Can Remember Your Past Lives. Robert C. Smith, under the editorship of Charles Thomas Cayce. Warner Books, New York, 1989.

Many Lives, Many Masters. Brian Weiss. Fireside Books, New York, 1988.

Other Lives, Other Selves: A Jungian Psychotherapist Discovers Past Lives. Roger J. Woolger, Ph.D. Bantam Books, New York, 1988.

Through Time into Healing. Brian Weiss. Simon & Schuster, New York, 1992.

Religion and Spirituality

Accept This Gift: Selections from a Course in Miracles. Frances Vaughan, Ph.D. and Roger Walsh, M.D., Ph.D. Jeremy Tarcher, Los Angeles, 1983.

Adam, Eve and the Serpent. Elaine Pagels. Random House, New York, 1988.

Bhagavad Gita. Translated by Swami Prabhavananda and Christopher Isherwood. Mentor (New American Library), New York, 1944.

A Course in Miracles. Foundation for Inner Peace, Farmingdale, New York, 1975.

Evil: The Shadow Side of Reality. John A. Sanford. The Crossroad Publishing Company, New York, 1989.

For the Love of God: New Writings by Spiritual and Psychological Leaders. Edited by Benjamin Shield and Richard Carlson, Ph.D. New World Library, San Rafael, California, 1990.

Global Mind Change. Willis Harman, Ph.D. Knowledge Systems, Inc., Indianapolis, Indiana, 1988.

The Gnostic Gospels. Elaine Pagels. Vintage Books, New York, 1981.

Hooked on God. Leo Booth. Jeremy Tarcher, Los Angeles, 1991.

In the Footsteps of Gandhi: Conversations with Spiritual Social Activists. Catherine Ingram. Parallax Press, Berkeley, California, 1990.

Jung and the Lost Gospels. Stephen A. Hoeller. Quest Books, Wheaton, Illinois, 1989.

Life's Companion: Journal Writing as a Spiritual Quest. Christina Baldwin. Bantam Books, New York, 1990.

Mister God, This Is Anna. Fynn. Ballantine Books, New York, 1974.

Original Blessing: A Primer in Creation Spirituality. Matthew Fox. Bear and Company, Sante Fe, New Mexico, 1983.

Peace Pilgrim: Her Life and Work in Her Own Words. Friends of Peace Pilgrim, 43480 Cedar Avenue, Hemet, California, 92344. Write for a free copy.

Recovering the Soul: A Scientific and Spiritual Search. Larry Dossey, M.D. Bantam Books, New York, 1990.

Returning: A Spiritual Journey. Dan Wakefield. Penguin Books, 1984.

The Sacred and the Profane: The Nature of Religion. Mircea Eliade. Harcourt, Brace, New York, 1959.

The Story of Your Life: Writing a Spiritual Autobiography. Dan Wakefield. Beacon Press, Boston, 1990.

The Upanishads. Translation and commentary by Swami Paramananda. Vedanta Centre Publishers, Cohasset, Massachusetts, 1981.

The Varieties of Religious Experience. William James. Mentor (New American Library), New York, 1958.

Meditation and Prayer

Book of Daily Thoughts and Prayers. Swami Paramananda. Vedanta Centre Publishers, Cohasset, Massachusetts, 1977.

Gratefulness, The Heart of Prayer. Brother David Steindl-Rast. Paulist Press, New York, 1984.

A Guide to Walking Meditation. Thich Nhat Hanh. Fellowship Publications, New York, 1985.

How to Know God: The Yoga Aphorisms of Patanjali. Translated with a new commentary by Swami Prabhavananda and Christopher Isherwood. Mentor (New American Library), New York, 1953.

Jewish Meditation: A Practical Guide. Aryeh Kaplan. Schocken Books, New York, 1985.

Meditations with Hildegard of Bingen. Gabrielle Uhlein. Bear and Company, Sante Fe, New Mexico, 1983.

Meditations with John of the Cross. Camille Campbell. Bear and Company, Sante Fe, New Mexico, 1989.

Meditations with Teilhard de Chardin. Blanche Gallagher. Bear and Company, Sante Fe, New Mexico, 1988.

Meditations with Teresa of Avila. Camille Campbell. Bear and Company, Sante Fe, New Mexico, 1985.

The Miracle of Mindfulness! A Manual of Meditation. Thich Nhat Hanh. Beacon Press, Boston, 1976.

Open Mind, Open Heart: The Contemplative Dimension of the Gospel. Thomas Keating. Amity House Press, New York, 1986. My absolute favorite book ever on meditation.

Outpouring of the Soul. Rabbi Nachman. Breslov Research Institute, Jerusalem, 1980.

Prayers of the Cosmos: Meditations on the Aramaic Words of Jesus. Neil Douglas-Klotz. Harper, San Francisico, 1990.

Restore My Soul. Rabbi Nachman. Breslov Research Institute, Jerusalem, 1980.

Poetry and Inspiration

A Book of Angels. Sophy Burnham. Ballantine Books, New York, 1990.

The Book of Job. Translated and with an introduction by Stephen Mitchell. North Point Press, San Francisco, 1987.

A Dancing Star: Inspirations to Guide and Heal. Eileen Campbell. The Aquarian Press (HarperCollins), New York, 1991.

Emmanuel's Book: A Manual for Living Comfortably in the Cosmos. Compiled by Pat Rodegast and Judith Santon. Bantam Books, New York, 1985.

Emmanuel's Book II: The Choice for Love. Compiled by Pat Rodegast and Judith Stanton. Bantam Books, New York, 1989.

The Enlightened Heart: An Anthology of Sacred Poetry. Edited by Stephen Mitchell. Harper & Row, New York, 1989.

An Interrupted Life: The Diaries of Etty Hillesum 1941–43. Etty Hillesum. Washington Square Press, New York, 1985.

The Kabir Book. Versions by Robert Bly. Beacon Press, Boston, 1971.

The Prophet. Kahlil Gibran. Knopf, New York, 1969.

Selected Poems and Plays. Rabindranath Tagore. Macmillan, New York, 1962.

Words to Love By. Mother Teresa. Ave Maria Press, Notre Dame, Indiana, 1983.

Men's Movement

Faces of the Enemy. Sam Keen. Harper & Row, New York, 1986.

Finding Our Fathers: The Unfinished Business of Manhood. Sam Osherson. Fawcett, New York, 1987.

Fire in the Belly: On Being a Man. Sam Keen. Bantam Books, New York, 1991.

Iron John. Robert Bly. Addison-Wesley, Boston, 1990.

The Intimate Connection: Male Sexuality, Masculine Spirituality. James B. Nelson. Westminster Press, Philadelphia, 1987.

Women's Spirituality

The Chalice and the Blade: Our History, Our Future. Riane Eisler. Harper & Row, San Francisco, 1987.

The Crone: Woman of Age, Wisdom and Power. Barbara G. Walker. Harper & Row, San Francisco, 1985.

The Feminine Face of God. Sherry Ruth Anderson and Patricia Hopkins. Bantam Books, New York, 1991.

The Song of Eve: An Illustrated Journey into the Myths, Symbols and Rituals of the Goddess. Manuela Dunn Mascetti. Simon & Schuster, New York, 1990.

Voices of Our Ancestors: Cherokee Teachings from the Wisdom Fire. Dhyani Ywahoo. Shambhala, Boston, 1987.

Woman as Healer. Jeanne Achterberg. Shambhala, Boston, 1990.

JOAN'S TAPES

In 1989 and 1990 I produced a set of seven guided meditation tapes entitled *Love Is the Lesson.* The tapes are enhanced by original music composed by Ultrasounds Studio™, except for *Healing the Inner Child,* which is set to Daniel Kobialka's deeply inspiring performance of Pachelbel's "Canon." The tapes are available singly or as a set and are identical on both sides, except for tapes 3 and 5, as indicated. Tapes available are:

1. Breath of Life, Breath of Love
2. Stretching and Relaxation
3. Concentration and Awareness (on sides A and B, respectively)
4. Gratitude and Healing Images
5. Healing the Inner Child (females on side A, males on side B)
6. Forgiveness and Healing Relationships
7. Rainbow Bridge: The Harmony of Opposites

Individual tapes are $8.95 each. The entire set is $54.95. Please include a check (or money order if you live outside the United States) made out to Mind/Body Health Sciences, Inc., for the amount of your order plus $2.75 for shipping and handling for one or two tapes, 10% of the cost of the order for more than two tapes. If you order by Visa or Mastercard include date of expiration. Please allow three to four weeks for delivery. Our address and telephone number are:

Mind/Body Health Sciences, Inc.
393 Dixon Rd.
Salina Star Route
Boulder, CO 80302

(303) 440–8460

We also publish an annual free newsletter called *Circle of Healing* that we would be delighted to send upon request.

MUSIC

In Dr. Larry Dossey's book *Meaning and Medicine: A Doctor's Stories of Breakthrough and Healing,* he discusses the remarkable work of a Japanese musician who assigned musical notes to the "base pairs" that constitute the DNA molecule. He then "played" the DNA of different cells, tissues and species. The music is remarkably similar to that of Mozart, Brahms and other great masters. Even the DNA of cancer cells has its own, beautiful melody. The echoes of divine harmony are implicit in much of the world's fine music. The following performances are some of my favorites. I have purposely left out most classical music, concentrating on lesser known or more specialized performances that you might like to explore.

Instrumental

The Music of Daniel Kobialka. Daniel Kobialka is a classical violinist who composes his own music and plays the old masters beautifully, often in half-time. His tapes are particularly evocative for guided imagery and provide peaceful backgrounds for meditation. Our favorites of his many cassettes are *Timeless Motion* (the Pachelbel "Canon" is on one side, two of Kobialka's compositions on the other) and *Path of Joy* ("Jesu, Joy of Man's Desiring" is on one side, two Kobialka compositions on the other).

Chaitanya Hari Deuter is a German musician who composes very interesting instrumental music with an Eastern influence, some of which has been used by public television. He has several cassettes, of which my favorites are *Cicada, Silence Is the Answer, Nirvana Road* and *San.*

Ray Lynch is a composer and musician who produces melodic, spirited, fun music of the synthesizer genre. *Deep Breakfast* is a classic.

The Source, by Osami Kitajima. The titles of the three long cuts on this CD are "Heavensent," "Thru Cosmic Doors" and "Eye to I." This is incredible music.

Atlantis Angelis is a melodic, meditative instrumental by Patrick Bernhart, with an occasional bit of magnificent chanting.

Santosh, by P. C. Davidoff. *Santosh* means "contentment." A delicate mix of harp and electronics, this music has distinct Eastern overtones and is deeply peaceful.

Vocal

A Feather on the Breath of God. Vocal compositions of the twelfth-century Christian mystic Abbess Hildegard of Bingen. These are similar to inspired Gregorian chants and are particularly uplifting, carrying the listener inward to silence.

Rhythm of Life. These inspired ecumenical spiritual songs were composed and performed by our neighbor Gordon Burnham. Myrin and I produced this cassette and sell it (for $10.95 plus $2.75 shipping and handling) through Mind/Body Health Sciences, Inc. (see page 229 for address). Guitar, flute, percussion, electronics and sweet vocal harmonies complement Gordon's rich voice.

Wheeler and Carol are a duo who compose, sing and perform uplifting spiritual music with a rhythm-and-blues feel. Their voices are deep and rich, the songs well-conceived and meaningful on their cassette *Mystic Soul*.

Singh Kaur and Kim Robertson: Mender of Hearts. This is a harp and vocal love song to the divine: "You are the mender of the heart, you are the sustainer of all. You are the mender of the wounds of life, you are the sustainer of all. . . ."

Robbie Gass and On Wings of Song. *Many Blessings* is a sampler of spiritually uplifting vocals. Their long chants *To the Goddess, Om Namah Shivaya, Hara Hara* and others create a peaceful, meditative atmosphere.

Rabbi David Zeller: The Path of the Heart. This is a live performance and sing-along. The acoustics aren't great and Zeller is not a professional musician, but the spirit is definitely there. We use many of these songs in our community healing circles.

Clannad: The Magical Ring. When my stepdaughter Natalia first heard this tape she stopped in her tracks halfway across the living room and closed her eyes, a blissful look on her face. When she "came to" her comment was, "What amazing music—like a choir of angels. I thought I'd died and gone to heaven."

Bobby McFerrin: Medicine Music. Master musician Bobby McFerrin (of "Don't Worry, Be Happy" fame) incites the listener to joy and reconnection with life.

Lisa Thiel combines a love of Eastern traditions with a love of the Native American culture in *Songs of the Spirit* and *Rising of the Phoenix*.

Enya weaves enchanting vocal harmonies around ancient Celtic melodies in *Enya* and *Shepherd Moons*.

Therése Schroeder-Sheker is a medieval scholar and musician with the voice and heart of an angel. *Rosa Mystica* is an album of ancient songs about the divine feminine. This is *the most* extraordinary music I have ever heard and been transformed by.

SPIRITUAL EMERGENCE NETWORK

The Spiritual Emergence Network was founded by Christina Grof in 1980. The need for such a network, which helps people to understand and find appropriate help for initiatory states that may mimic psychiatric emergencies, is attested to by its rapid growth into an international information, education and referral service for people who are in the midst of transformative experiences. The network's address and telephone number are:

The Institute of Transpersonal Psychology
250 Oak Grove Avenue
Menlo Park, CA 94025

(415) 327-2776

As mentioned earlier, when seeking referral to any kind of practitioner, use both your logic and your intuition. When in doubt, a second opinion usually helps.

PAST-LIFE THERAPY

The following individuals offer either seminars and training for professionals or individual therapy.

Morris Netherton, Ph.D.
Star Center
Associated Healing Arts, Inc.
Suite 318, Ruxton Towers
8415 Bellona Lane
Towson, MD 21204

(410) 321-0777

Roger Woolger, Ph.D.
Woolger Training Seminars
5 River Road
New Paltz, New York 12561

(914) 658-8617

Brian Weiss, M.D.
9100 South Dadeland Boulevard, Suite 1400
Miami, FL 33156

(305) 670-0410

ORGANIZATIONS AND PUBLICATIONS

The Institute of Noetic Sciences. The Institute was founded by astronaut Edgar Mitchell as the result of a profound "holy moment" when he stood on the moon and looked back at our jewel-like planet. The Institute reports research and education on human consciousness. Its goal is "to broaden knowledge of the nature and potentials of mind and consciousness, and to apply that knowledge to the enhancement and quality of life on the planet." The Institute publishes a fascinating quarterly journal, *The Noetic Sciences Review*. It also publishes summaries of its excellent research in such areas as psychoneuroimmunology, multiple personality disorder, spontaneous remission, healings at Lourdes, creative altruism and other areas involving mind, body and consciousness. Write to the Institute of Noetic Sciences, 475 Gate 5 Road, Suite 300, Sausalito, CA 94965.

The John E. Fetzer Institute. This visionary institute is a leader in research and education of the connection between bodymind and spirit. It has recently taken over publication of the journal *Advances* from the Institute for the Advancement of Health. The quarterly journal *Advances* is packed with scholarly articles on the bodymind by noted scientists, physicians and other researchers. It also abstracts the literature in behavioral medicine, psychoneuroimmunology and the psychology of health and illness. Aimed primarily at a professional audience, *Advances* is nonetheless excellent reading for the interested layperson. Write to the John E. Fetzer Institute, 1292 West KL Avenue, Kalamazoo, MI 49009.

The Spindrift Foundation. Spindrift is a nondenominational Christian group that does highly rigorous research on prayer, "exploring prayer and healing through the experimental test." They publish an occasional newsletter that is fascinating but often highly technical. They also make their voluminous research data available to the public. Write to Spindrift, Inc., P.O. Box 5134, Salem, OR 97304-5134.

New Age Journal. This magazine has really blossomed under the new senior editor, one of the magazine's original founders, Peggy Taylor. Lively, informative and very well grounded, the magazine is full of resources and ideas for healing ourselves and our planet. Available on the newsstand or by subscription. Write to New Age Journal, P.O. Box 53275, Boulder CO 80321-3275.

Yoga Journal. While the name seems somewhat limiting since many people think of yoga as primarily a system of physical exercises, *Yoga Journal* is a first-class publication featuring excellent interviews and articles about the broadest range of healing. Look for wonderful interviews and editorials by senior editor Stephan Bodian. Available on the newsstand or by subscription. Write to Yoga Journal, P.O. Box 3755, Escondido, CA 92033.

Common Boundary: The Interface Between Spirituality and Psychotherapy. This is an up-and-coming magazine that does exactly what it intends—acts as an interface between disciplines that have grown apart and desperately need to be reunited. It also sponsors an annual conference that draws a wide range of professionals and interested laypeople. Write to Common Boundary Circulation Office, 8528 Bradford Road, Silver Spring, MD 20815.

Creation: Earthy Spirituality. *Creation* is published by Dominican priest Matthew Fox's organization and concerns the subject of creation spirituality, a spiritually optimistic, celebratory theology that hopes to advance the new cosmology now being articulated by scientists, psychologists and clergy. Write to Subscription Department, Creation Magazine, 160 Virginia Street #290, San Jose, CA 95112.

The Quest is a quarterly magazine published by the American Theosophical Society. "The journal is dedicated to an exploration of a worldview which embraces ideas of wholeness and compassion, and which seeks to draw on the divine wisdom which is found in all religious traditions, and is often called 'the perennial philosophy.'" Write to The Quest, P.O. Box 270, Wheaton, IL 60189-0270.

Gnosis: A Journal of the Western Inner Traditions. *Gnosis* is published quarterly by the Lumen Foundation. It invites the reader to "explore the inner traditions of the West. . . . We're dedicated to presenting highly readable intelligent information on the esoteric spiritual paths that are present in our own backyard . . . material that is hard to find in any other journal." Write to Gnosis Magazine, P.O. Box 14217, San Francisco, CA 94114-0217.

Parabola: Myth and the Quest for Meaning. This quarterly journal is a feast for the eyes as well as the soul. Magnificent art, fascinating articles and short stories as teaching tales make every issue a delight. Write to Parabola, 656 Broadway, New York, NY 10012-2317.

Wingspan: Journal of the Male Spirit. This quarterly journal of the emerging men's movement is packed with articles, ideas, resources, workshop information and the like. It also provides opportunities to find men's groups in your area and a calendar of men's events. Write to Wingspan, Box 1491, Manchester, MA 01944.

Woman of Power: A Magazine of Feminism, Spirituality and Politics. This quarterly magazine of women's spirituality "seeks to generate harmony and interconnection by taking care that our words and images nurture and affirm our wholeness. We honor artworks, writings and activities which enable us to transform our fears into loving, affirming actions." Write to Woman of Power, P.O. Box 827, Cambridge, MA 02238.

ReVision: The Journal of Consciousness and Change. This quarterly magazine is edited by three leaders of the consciousness movement, Stanislav Grof, Ralph Metzner and Huston Smith. The articles are of scholarly quality, yet highly readable. Write to ReVision, Heldref Publications, 400 Albemarle Street NW, Washington, DC 20016.

New Sense Bulletin has been a companion of ours for years. (Until recently it was called *Brain Mind Bulletin*. A newsletter conceived of and published by the visionary Marilyn Ferguson, whose book *The Aquarian Conspiracy* is a classic, *New Sense* is a must for keeping abreast of research news, happenings and interesting books. Write to New Sense Bulletin, P.O. Box 42211, Los Angeles, CA 90042.

Fellowship in Prayer has been published since 1949. Thoroughly and delightfully ecumenical, it comes out six times a year. The February 1991 issue, for example, contained an article on impermanence by a Tibetan lama, an article on the silent dimension of Islam, an article on prayer of the heart by a rabbi, an article on transformation that occurred from facing a major illness, poetry from the Iroquois nation, poetry from readers and a column of great quotations called "Insights." Write to Fellowship in Prayer, 291 Witherspoon Street, Princeton, NJ 08542.

I hope that some of the resources in this chapter will help you realize your highest vision of what you can be—and reassure you that the divine seed of that being is already present within you, watered as it is by the crises and difficulties of this wondrous and mysterious life.

PERMISSIONS